Helene

THE FAI

illustrations by Antonio Lupatelli
and Richard Doyle

The Fairy Tarot
© 2004 by Lo Scarabeo.

First English Edition
First printing, 2004

Italian Title: Tarocchi dei Folletti

By Helene Saltarini
Cover image by Antonio Lupatelli
Illustrations by Antonio Lupatelli and Richard Doyle

Translation by Liz O'Neill

Editing and book design:
Pietro Alligo, Riccardo Minetti, Alberto Gedda, Arnell Ando

Printed in the EU

Lo Scarabeo S.r.l.
Via Varese 15c 10152 - Torino - Italy
info@loscarabeo.com - www.loscarabeo.com

ISBN 88 8395 423-8

Helene Saltarini

THE FAIRY TAROT

Illustrations by Antonio Lupatelli
and Richard Doyle

LO SCARABEO

INDEX

INTRODUCTION

The Fairy Tarot has a particular begining. The story is told in fact, that the Great Magician of the Enchanted Kingdom – a vast territory rich with ancient forests, waterfalls and lakes inhabited by Fairies – went to the Emperor and Empress with a proposal to assist them in governing their People, who were undisciplined, rambunctious and unruly. In order to understand the preoccupation of the Magician and the rulers, it is necessary to know that the Fairies are magical creatures, winged sprites that love to pass their days happily, contriving pranks to play on others, at the expense of those caught in their sights, never with evil intentions but only to vent their natural restlessness and exhuberance.

In his old age the Magician had acquired great experience and wisdom. One day he heard an interesting piece of information while conversing with a gnome, who was related to him. The Gnomes could actually be considered cousins of the Fairies. They are also magical creatures, but not winged and are of a more serious and reflective nature. The Gnome was talking about the Tarot: he was discussing a system he himself had invented, comprising 78 cards onto which he had transfered his experiences and wisdom. These he used to look into the future and give advice to his kinfolk, assisting them to act in the best way regarding the various circumstances of life. Why not try the same method with the Fairies, to help them understand all they need to know to live their lives better while captivating their curiosity.

Years passed from the Magician's proposal to its actual implementation, but the result was very rewarding. The artists who created these cards managed to combine in their illustrations the traditions of the Fairies, their habits and customs, with images that are easy to understand and to recall, and that speak directly to the heart.

Furthermore the Magician gave them the power to be arranged in particular combinations, that refelceted the various situations in which the Fairies could find themselves. In this way it was easy to follow the advice given by the cards regarding how to behave in the diverse situations of life.

It is not certain if the idea of the Tarots was really that of the Wizard of the Gnomes or the Magican of the Fairies. It actually seems that the members of the Little People (who are divided into multiple species, all similar even if notably diverse amongst themselves) have the inveterate habit of imitating humans, frequently borrowing their habits and customs.

The similarity between our classic Tarots and the Fairy Tarot is notable, and in both cases the language of the symbols is so strong that it penetrates our soul and cannot be forgottten.

The Tarot can be defined as magical cards for their symbolism that reveals to us a richer and broader dimension of life than normal, and that help us to

9

examine our unconscious and to better understand ourselves. They also help us to find an equilibrium, new persepctives and harmony with those that we hold dear. The illuminating pages written on the Tarot are faithful to many esoteric scholars, one of whom was Oswald Wirth, a great man of learning who designed and published in 1889 a series of 22 drawings that he named the Major Arcana. Another equally important person was Arthur Edward Waite, to whom we are indebted for a famous deck, designed following his instructions in the Liberty style, and published in 1910, also in England. Both are invaluable guides to better understanding the fascinating symbolism of these cards.

Belief in the magical Fairy people has been lost over time. Their tradition is in fact thousands of years old: the earliest wooden statues that depict them date from 1200 B.C., verified by scientific tests conducted on them.

In many parts of the world the testimonies and knowledge that revolve around the mystery of the Fairies are numerous and often jealously guarded. Also in our country legends connected to the Little People abound, from those of Monte Bianco and the Dolomites to that of Monte Cònero near Ancona. Undoubtably however it is the Nordic countries and above all England and Ireland, who conserve and pass down the most ancient and significant testimonies.

In one of the inumerable legends from these countries, it is told that in the vicinity of a lake exists a mysterious door to the kingdom of the Fairies. It opens only once a year, on the first of May, after the magic feast for the "Night of Valpurga". Whoever enters, challenges fate, both those who sneak in and those who are invited. The Fairies are in fact jealous of their secrets and there are very few mortals who have returned with their senses intact and who wish to reccount their experiences.

The scarse testimonies, ancient records and legends that exist all describe the Fairies as supernatural beings, gifted with magic power; generally pranksters who live in the ancient forests, the waterfalls or the rocks and caverns, and who belong to a very unified and exclusive race, a "clan", distinguished by it's very way of being. They prefer to wear green-coloured clothes, or to be covered in flowers and leaves in order to blend with and be better hidden by the leaves of the forest. They are very intrigued by people, but do not like to be seen by them. They love to dance in the wooded glades and the clearings, and above all by the light of the moon.

It is difficult to see Fairies, because they are extremely small. They are as tall as an outstretched palm, weigh about as much in proportion, but they are at least seven times stronger than a healthy man. They are not immortal, but they have a very long life, which can last up to four centuries.

10

There is a distinct difference between the inhabitants in their world that makes it difficult to establish to what group a Fairy belongs as even their naming is complicated. The same "types" of one category can in fact have different names according to the region they live in, so that in one place a Fairy is called Bogie and in another, even one nearby, Bogle. There are no logical rules for the terminology.

Pixies, or Green Fairies, often take the shape of porcupines, which is the image used for the Ace of Leaves in their Tarot: they are hard workers and often thresh the wheat at night to have in compensation bread and cheese-their prefered food- from mortals. Pixies are also known as Pisgie or Piskie, according to the regions they live in. The Phooka however is an Irish Fairy that can, according to legend, assume the form of various animals.

Fairies are disrespectful but not particularly bad, apart from Trolls who are all bad and who tend to dwell in the rocks. The Brownies group are good Fairies who willingly help humans in their buisness in return for a bowl of cream or some honey.

In our technological age, Fairies are discussed less and less, such that most people laugh when asked if they believe in the existence of these magical creatures.

Nevertheless many of us are convinced that on this planet and in the universe other things also exist, even if invisible to us.

When one investigates these sprites one remains confused; it is hard to know what to believe in or not. In fact there are actually numerous legends, various descriptions, written and oral traditions handed down over the course of the centuries in different countries, and many contradict others.

Without concrete or certain proof, an attempt was made to place the Fairies in the realm of fables, but a doubt remains. Can such an ancient tradition be based only on fantasy?

With this in mind, it is timely to recall that during the last century, in Germany, a certain Mr Schliemannn lived, who greatly loved the poems of Homer and maintained they were not just a poetic invention. Schliemann dedicated his life searching for Troy, the city described in the Illiad, heedless of those who took him for a poor deluded fool. His faith was rewarded by the rediscovery of the city and the treasure of it's King Priamo, which was the stuff of legends for over three thousand years.

A friend of ours has recounted that in her region, the south of Italy, they still talk today of the fables and the various legends regarding the mysterious Fairies.

One of these is very much ingrained in popular culture. It tells of a female Fairy, whose name is unknown, who had the habit of sitting on the stom-

11

ach of a sleeping person. If this person awoke because of the weight they felt, and realised that they were in the presence of a Fairy, they had to immeadiately pull out one of her hairs. The Fairy, in order to have her hair returned, had to grant three wishes, which the person had to express immediately.

If the sleeper however did not realise that there was a Fairy present, they would have lost a great opportunity. Still today in that place it happens that people, perhaps with problems, are heard to exclaim: "If a Fairy should happen to sit on my stomach, I certainly will not let such good luck escape".

Another friend has recounted her own experience as a child, with a Fairy. She was six and it was her birthday. The sun was hot even though the autumn equinox was close, and shone through the wooden shutters creating a beautiful game of light between the orderly white blinds close to her bed. She was excited and decided to enjoy this magical spectacle, even though she knew that in the lounge she would find a present from her parents. From one side, high up on the curtain, twelve small Fairies that seemed to be made of silver light, began to descend, swinging between the curtains, forming little circles and doing cartwheels. Astonished, she rubbed her eyes but the Fairies were still there, dancing and laughing for her. "My mother", said the friend, " entered the room at that moment to wish me happy birthday, and when I looked back at the curtains they were not there any longer. That was the only time that I ever saw them and still today, many many years later, on the morning of my birthday I look at that same window, hoping to see them again. Nevertheless, who knows....maybe it's not their purpose anymore...they may be celebrating the birthday of another child".

Basically, there is nothing wrong in remaining connected to the legends even as an adult and to consider the Fairies a reality.

Little by little as one becomes familiar with the Enchanted Kingdom and it's inhabitants and becomes therefore more involved in their world and enters into harmony with them, one feels more supported, guided and comforted by their magic presence. The Fairy Oracle can give you the correct answer to your doubts, help you solve problems involving loved ones, by providing comprehensive advice to all. To understand oneself better, one needs to also be more understanding of those close to us.

The chapter entitled " the divinatory systems" explains how to interrogate these magical creatures in order to receive the correct answers.

Kind readers, we wish you wonderful responses from the oracle you consult.

12

THE MAJOR ARCANA

THE ELF – ARCANA 0

This card depicts the Elf, a typical representative of his people, happy and a little crazy, who makes a joke of the rules and who is always ready to play tricks on everyone, for his own enjoyment. He can be seen in fact playing a tambourine. Next to him is a trombone. There is also a small sylvan animal, similar to the wolf of the classical Tarot, who tugs the Elf by his shirt and tries to stop him from giving free reign to all his instincts and egotistical temptations, and to anchor him to reality. The Elf however leaps, laughs and plays nonetheless, spellbound by the full moon.

Pay attention to the moon in the sky: it is particuarly unpredictable, appearing removed from material things. It changes day by day and makes one fol-

15

low unrealizable dreams, while right now it is important for the seeker to be more stable and focused.

If this card appears during a consultation, one can choose to either take life as a challenge, swaying back and forth on the edge of a precipice without any precise destination; or one can try to intuit what is behind the game and to aim towards the objectives that one wishes to accomplish. This is a well-defined road and can be achieved only after certain difficulties have been overcome. The Elf Arcana, number 0 of 22, could be the begining or the end of the Major Arcana, as it is the connecting link between the Magician/1, the first Arcana, and the World/22, the last. This means that if one has extracted this powerful card one will be able to reunite the broken cords, repair spoiled relationships, recommence interrupted projects. The Elf represents chaos, which one needs to know how to keep in order, carefully interpreting the cards that accompany it.

Upright: even if you have made a mistake, fortune will assist you.

Reversed: a tendency to create professional and economic problems.

16

THE MAGICIAN – ARCANA I

This card shows the Magician, an important Fairy, of great knowledge and initiative.

The Magician is in an alchemic laboratory, his dominion. If you have chosen this card it means that right now you are the Magician. Your magic powers are active and you are not without the means to realize your desires.

In front is a table on which the objects of his magic art are placed: the crystal ball for looking into the future; the magic wand to grant and realize wishes; the vessels that contain the potions and the miraculous water used for spells; the stone for providing concreteness; the cube to attain perfection in every action. You have many instruments at your disposal, in particular

17

astuteness and the art of diplomacy, to direct your life in the desired direction.

On the table the four primitive elements can also be found: the cube comes from the Earth element, the containers from Water, the wand from Air and the element of Fire is contained within the crystal ball.

The tall Magician's hat, covered in stars, represents his link with the heavens. This signifies not having limits and that you can aim high for the realization of your goals. You may have valuable inspirations, because you are in harmony with the Universe.

Behind the Magician is a nocturnal bird, the owl, loved by both witches and magicians, who use it as a messenger. If you are not afraid of it, it will bring you fortune.

The Magician has enormous power and abilities, and is full of initiatives. He is loyal if you believe in him; if you are sceptical of his art however then you should be wary of his magic, as it can be both good and evil.

Upright: do not look for help elsewhere: you will do better on your own.

Reversed: be careful not to count on the wrong person; listen to the Magician in you!

THE HIGH PRIESTESS – ARCANA II

This Fairy takes us into the sacred kingdom. The High Priestess is acknowledged for her wisdom and her kindness towards all, but she is also feared for her severe judgement which is often seen by the carefree Fairies as a hinderance to their freedom.

The High Priestess is gifted with great intelligence and dedicated to the occult sciences, and is the absolute Pontiff of her own opinions. She can help you realize your aspirations through consistancy, discipline and faith in higher powers.

The High Priestess wears a tall hat, a symbol of strength. On her breast she wears a five-pointed star, a pentagram with the apex at the top. These sym-

19

bols represent her power over the primitive elements: fire, water, earth and air, and the fifth element that keeps all the others in equilibrium. She tells you to be a little self-critical, more introspective, with the aim of distributing your energies more equally in all areas of life.

This sacred Fairy, like the Sphinx, holds in her hand the Book of Wisdom. She allows into her kingdom only those who know how to give a just reply to her questions, which are written in a book held by a large and kindly toad. In the same way you will find the answers to your problems, using wise intuition.

A beautiful peacock with its tail spread open expresses the pride of this Fairy, a defect which you may also expressing. Be careful not to exaggerate!

On the cover of the book is the symbol of Venus, of love and eternal life. The Fairies live for centuries and are giving you too the gift of a long life.

Upright: represents a dear and faithful person that you care about; It also signifies that the heavens protect you.

Reversed: you realize that you have made a wrong choice; try to remedy this.

THE EMPRESS – ARCANA III

This Fairy, the wife of the Emperor, has great power over the lives of the Fairies. As she is very understanding and always willing to help others, everyone wants her friendship and kindness. This ruler represents female compassion and creative intelligence, corresponding to the sacred waters that contain the secrets of birth.

This card corresponds to the Goddess Isis from the Egyptian tradition. She prohibits entry into the temple of those who are not ready to learn certain mysteries.

If you have extracted this card you are invited to open the door of the Temple of your heart to your conscience, to altruism and to spirituality.

21

We see the Empress with a crown garnished with various bells and with a tall hat, which the most magical Fairies possess. She demonstrates an inborn stately attitude of a certain rigidity. Her gaze penetrates but is not hostile. With one hand she holds the hilt of sword, ready to command or to defend. On the back of the other hand the Empress's messenger, a falcon, sits. This is a warning: you also have a mission to accomplish, but you have yet to discover what.

At her feet is a casket overflowing with precious objects, symbol of the riches she bestows on those whom she considers to merit them. Finally you will be compensated for your efforts!

The casket is next to the roots of a great tree, and almost seems to be a part of the tree. This is a sign that you need to restore the spirit with the treasures of nature, forgetting the problems of daily life for a while.

Upright: this Fairy guarantees her support, but will wait for your first move. You are resourceful and sure of yourself, therefore make the first move.

Reversed: to get what you want you must direct yourself with courage and strength towards a new road. Find the strength to overturn the currently uncertain situation.

THE EMPEROR – ARCANA IV

The Emperor is the ruler of the Enchanted Kingdom of the Fairies. Bestowed with great will, he represents law and order, but he has much to do as his people are rather undisciplined and disorderly. You also must give your desires some order and prioritize your aims.

The Emperor corresponds to the Demiurge of the Platonics and to the Great Architect of the Masons' Universe. Extracting this card signifies that you also could have a "small demiurge" in various aspects of life, to whom you turn for the best advice.

In the card the Emperor is seated on an unusual throne, strangely marked, with the symbol of a wheel incised above, that indicates the

23

constant circular movements of the earth and sky.

Under the throne two small animals are hiding. They feel protected by the Emperor, exactly the same way his people feel protected. Leaning on the throne is a large sword, always ready to punish the guilty.

In his right hand the Emperor holds the spectre of command. He has his head covered by a helmet-crown, on the top of which can be seen a small dragon. Both items symbolize the absolute power of the Fairy. A gigantic eagle, the symbol of integrity and dignity, rests his wings on the back of the throne, in harmony with the Emperor. It is an incentive for you to be confident and reflective.

This card advises that the moment has arrived to make a decision, but do not hurry: evaluate calmly the pros and cons.

The Emperor corresponds to the IV Arcana, which expresses both the earthly plane and the spiritual plane: the natural world where the Fairies live and work, but also the fusion of one with the other.

Upright: create order in a chaotic situation, even if this costs fatigue and effort, as you do not want schematic situations.

Reversed: if you do not heed the warning to order of the Emperor, you will find yourself in a lot of trouble!

THE HIEROPHANT or HIGH PRIEST – ARCANA V

The High Priest is the most sacred person of the Fairies. It is he who possesses the key to the High Magic. He has the difficult job of responding to every anxious question from his Fairies, to pour over them the water of life from the heavens, even if they frequently do not immeadiately understand, as they are capricious and stubborn.

This card indicates that often you too want to do things your own way, a defect that sometimes hinders you from demonstrating your best qualities. The Hierophant is smiling kindly. In his hand he holds a shepherds staff and the scared book of law is open, visible to all, with two engraved keys for interpretation, that allow him to enter into areas forbidden to common Fairies.

25

Extracting this card means that an opening is appearing for you, the possibility to follow a special path, little known to others.

The books and the parchment placed under his feet indicate the knowledge of the High Priest, and his long beard reveals his infinite wisdom. These are the tools that you should use in this moment of your life.

The High Priest knows to search both on land and in the sky, and is the bridge between high and low. Next to him we see a nest with three eggs, that represent the latent powers that can be brought to light. This signifies that there are unacknowledged talents harbouring in you.

To his right there is a regal cat, in an attentive pose, who acts as his assistant. The primitive energy of this animal unites with the cosmic energy. The Hierophant has the power to help you find the point of union between your emotional and rational nature. His large pointed ears signify that he knows to listen, even when nothing is being said.

Upright: this will be useful in the realisation of your intentions.

Reversed: always try to pave the road in order to walk serenely, however you need to believe in yourself, to have faith.

THE LOVERS – ARCANA VI

This lovely picture is in actual fact a little worrying for the carefree Fairy who wants to have fun and not to assume any great responsibility, above all in love. Very reluctantly does she or he want to be tied to someone for the rest of his/her life.

Initially, the card appears to offer a simple interpretation: you have met the person that makes your heart beat faster, or you are aspiring to a great love. In reality you are in front of a kind of Karmic test, in the choice of the person you want next to you, a turning point that destiny proposes, linked to the degree of understanding and spirituality attained.

In the center of the card, on a flower, we see two lovers who hold each others' hands. The couple is surrounded by delicate white flowers,a symbol of the emotional purity that you are feeling in your heart.

It is up to you to understand or intuit, if you are dealing with a fleeting physical attraction or with true love. Pure love is a creative act, altruistic; it is moved by observing the opening of a flower and sees the best side in everyone.

This Arcana in fact, according to ancient traditions, refers to love for all humanity, for every created thing, and not only the falling in love with a single individual. Extracting this cards signifies that this is the moment for you to open your heart to all types of love, the most universal: towards nature, towards other human beings, and in daily life.

Upright: this Fairy will oblige you to make a decision, a precise choice, but be calm: the Arcana will protect you.

Reversed: the choice will be a dilemma and, if you do not evaluate the emotional situation carefully, you could easily make a mistake.

THE CHARIOT – ARCANA VII

This Arcana is also called the Chariot of Triumph, because following a challenge, the winner passes proudly past the Fairies, showing his success to all. This is an extermely positive card, promising great victories in any enterprise. Have faith in your ideas and projects, realize them now!

We see that the chariot does not have its' wheels on the ground, but rather is suspended in air; thus we are dealing with an arial parade, indicating great glory and honour. The chariot is pulled by six winged beasts that are looking around them with pride and arrogance, to ensure that all can see their triumphant pass.

29

The Victorious Fairy represents the Antimony of the Basilio Valentino. Otherwise known as the spirit who fights for his evolution, he puts on his armour and grips a spear which he holds up high to be easily seen, aimed towards the heavens. In his other hand he holds a shield in the form of a shining sun, radiating joy and power.

If you have extracted this card, the moment has arrived to give room to the ideas and hopes that you have probably kept hidden in a closet, being too busy with the struggle of daily life.

Be careful however before you cry victory, as you could easily attract jealousy and envy.

Keep in mind that even if this card promises success in all areas, it depends on you to maintain it by your behaviour. It is difficult to climb the high summits but much easier to slide down to the valleys below.

Upright: this Arcana does not only indicate the achievement or the success of a project, but above all personal triumph, which will bring you glory and immense satisfaction.

Reversed: this Fairy requests that you achieve your objectives with diplomacy and without haste, otherwise obstacles could appear that would delay the outcome.

THE DRYAD – ARCANA VIII

This Fairy represents the spirit of justice. Her task is to listen to the controversies of her people and to help them by expressing her opinion. Once asked for, her verdict must be accepted without debate.

The time has arrived to become more aware, to not face life soley with the lightheartedness that is so dear to the Fairies. A pinch of seriousness will be of value, without taking away the joy of life!

The Dryad, who lives near a giant oak, is kneeling on a book of Laws, placed on a great mushroom, and only she knows its contents. She holds a scale, the bowls in perfect equilibrium, to weigh the deeds and misdeeds of the Fairies. In her other hand she has a sword with the tip aimed upwards.

31

Her eyes are blindfolded; she has no need to see as she follows her inner voice. The wings of the nymphs of the woods are beautiful, reflecting blue lights, and are straight, a sign of pride and dignity. Remember: your actions will be carefully evaluated. Important consequences for the future derive from them.

Completely naked as the truth, the Dryad has only a magic hat on her head, covered with precious stones and pearls at the top. This Arcana advises you to always act frankly, because deception and tricks will only create disappointments.

The Dryad represents the end of an uncertain and chaotic situation and the begining of another road, more orderly and clear.

She is a hicratic Fairy, symbol of both nature and the Karmic Laws: every human being receives only that which they deserve and construct.

Upright: it is opportune to resolve any arguments or legal issues, to clarify one's real opinion with honest dialogue.

Reversed: you could have an injustice done to you or become unhappy due to lack of comprehension from a person who is dear to you.

THE HERMIT – ARCANA IX

The Hermit is a particular Fairy, because he tries to distance himself from the others. He does not do this out of spite or haughtiness but because he is a thinker, a Wise One, whose advice everyone willingly heeds. The Fairies respect him, however they do not feel comfortable with him as he is so serious and can say so much just in a glance.

This Fairy represents the Genie, trapped in the lamp, that would like to spread his knowledge amongst the others but instead arouses dread, and apprehension, as not everyone can understand him.

In the card we see an elderly Fairy inside the trunk of a tree, from where only his head pokes out. In his hand he holds a lantern alight, which repre-

33

sents the inner conscience. It recalls the lamp of Diogene, that searched for humankind, but the true being we can find only within ourselves. His lamp which is lit in the dead of night, and with which he searches to see if there is another like him, radiates its light to no avail.

He also has a book in front of him. It is the book of wisdom, where illuminating answers can be found to every question.

The Hermit is also compared to Saturn, the Master of the occult, whose magic square is composed of nine compartments which are organised in the correct position in order that the sum of their numbers is always 15 in all directions. Not without reason, patience is a virtue of the Wise Ones.....

Upright: if you are unsure of where to turn, look for inner calm and trust the suggestion of this Fairy, even if it appears difficult to follow.

Reversed: you are lost in pessimism and mistrust, but this is unnecessary. With intropection a breath of hope will arise, while impulsiveness may well make you regret your decision.

THE OREAD – ARCANA X

The Oread is the spirit of Fortune, that travels through this Kingdom spell-bound, pedaling on her wheel. All the fairies hope to meet her by chance for she brings good fortune.

The Oread brings riches and bestows to each what they desire above all else and can enrich with money or sentiments, filling the heart with joy.

The card shows this Fairy on a wheel, pedaling happily with her nose in the air, while joyously breathing in the magic scents of the woods and feeling at one with all. Everything about the Oread speaks of abundance and in fact this card is also called the Wheel of Fortune.

Remember that everything has a positive and a negative side, and therefore even fortune can hide a danger. You are aware of this and do not squander it, but also know to grasp fortune when it passes quickly by. This Fairy promises a thousand fruits of every kind and does not give preference to anyone

The Oread equally dispenses to each their own. What we take however without merit will sooner or later be taken from us.

Upright: triumph of fortune; joyful news from everywhere will reach you and above all you will feel strong and happy inside, and will not forget those who have need of you.

Reversed: Attention, do not immediately accept everything that is offered to you in abundance, but choose and evaluate each situation carefully. Think also of its development and not only of the present moment.

STRENGTH – ARCANA XI

The Fairy of Strength is continually controlling the strength within him by ripping out the heaviest trees in the woods. He renounces amusements and games, concerned only about increasing his power, not only physical power but also psychic power. Anyone can go to him for advice or for moral and practical support for a just cause.

In this card a huge tree can be seen, one that has been growing for hundreds of years. The Fairy has just uprooted it ,even though he is so small he cannot even put his arms around it. Even the branches of the tree are enormous; some stretching up to the sky. The wings of the Fairy are closed so that they do not get entangled in the branches. His precious helmet seems to possess

37

a magical force, as it is not damaged by the tree but appears to actually hold it up.

The tree is dead. The Fairy has eliminated it to make space for a new tree: just as we should have the strength of spirit to eliminate what can no longer bear fruit.

The number 11 of the Arcana is compose of two number one's placed close together. They reveal therefore the two essential principles of all of nature, without which nothing can be created. To give birth to something, a male and a female principle are required. Only in this way can the physical and the spiritual unite. Our strong and wise Fairy knows this well. In fact many traditions talk about the power that has it's mysterious strength, if it is well directed and used for the good of others.

Upright: you are filled with strength, security and decisions: start working. Reversed: great physical and psychological strength could also overwhelm you and make you over-estimate your capabilities. Do not immediately uproot the trees. Think about it first, before ending up half-way there.

THE MAJOR ARCANA

THE HANGED MAN – ARCANA XII

The Fairies allow themselves many pranks and games, some more serious than other. However when they go over the limit they are punished by those who have the responsibility to dispense justice and maintain order. This card always indicates a serious situation: sacrifices need to be made to exit from the tunnel, and no-one else can do this for us.

In this card we see a guilty Fairy, hung by a foot from the trunk of a tree, with his head down and his beautiful wings dirty. Until they are cleaned he will not be able to fly. This represents an enormous displeasure for the Fairy, as flying is his great joy. Only the left leg is free, bent above the right to form a cross. This position obliges him to think and reflect on how to

39

THE MAJOR ARCANA

remedy his guilt. As such the Fairy resembles the Nordic god Odin, who sacrificed himself for nine nights and nine days, hanging upside down from the tree of knowledge, to enable this knowledge to penetrate.

A snake is coiled around the arm of the Fairy, representing the sacred serpent that wishes to guide him to higher knowledge. In his other hand he has an empty bag of his earthly belongings which have fallen to the ground. The Fairy can appeal only to his inner strength to be reborn and to be conscious of the cosmic laws.

This card, which on first sight appears negative, in reality represents a positive fact. It teaches that with knowledge and true will you can reach the highest point. If you lack inner strength however, you will remain "hung".

Upright: an act of altruism or maturity, will take you down a new road, even if initially this will not be easy. Avoid fixed ideas; the mind needs to be open.

Reversed: sudden obstacles will impede you from reaching your pre-defined objectives. Be patient; it is important that you know to knock on other doors and to ask for assistance humbly.

DEATH – ARCANA XIII

This Arcana represents death, which almost everyone is afraid of, including both Fairies and humans. This does not represent physical death, but more the end of something or a radical change. The Fairy that sees this spirit could be obliged to leave his or her home and land and begin again elsewhere. This Arcana therefore indicates difficult changes rather than actual death.

The Fairies know that death, as mortals invision it to be, does not exist. The spirit is immortal and lives from one reincarnation to another and earthly experiences bring with them a constant spiritual growth. We only abandon the "clothes of the spirit", the body, and not the Divine essence that is in each of us.

The image that we see is Death, which moves through the forest, searching for whoever has to leave the earth. The sinister light of the moon renders the scene even more spectral.

Everyone is silent. The usual laughter of the disrespectful Fairies is unheard. No-one is around, as everyone has taken refuge in their homes, hoping not to be met by the ghostly apparition. Even though the Fairies enjoy a very long life, they greatly fear this Fairy.

The number 13 of this Arcana is generally feared. Even some hotels do not have a room with this number, as no-one wishes to sleep in it. Others however consider this number fortunate: it depends on one's point of view of things. Nothing is unilateral.

Upright: something in your life will undergo change: this could be a good thing for you. It could liberate you from something that was weighing heavily for some time.

Reversed: you lack trust, have dark thoughts, could loose something or finish a love affair. You need to act with a strong spirit when faced with obstacles and over time some of these may well turn out to be positive.

THE MAJOR ARCANA

THE SYLPH – ARCANA XIV

The Sylph is much loved amongst the Fairies because she is always gentle and flexibile which are rare virtues amongst them. She is also considered the Spirit of Healing, and has many surpises in store for everyone. The Fairies therefore willingly speak with her, enriching themselves with her wisdom and her gifts.

We see the Sylph merrily flying above a heavily wooded part of the forest, holding an amphora in each hand, from which she dispenses the colours of the rainbow: from one come the infrared colours, from the other, ultraviolet. These colours, the so-called hot and cold colours, are mixed together in the rainbow which is a gift of nature to all living creatures, and promises joy

43

and health. The healing powers of the rainbow have been believed in for aeons. The leaves, mushrooms and flowers are all turned upwards, giving the impression that they are absorbing the positive rays of the magic rainbow poured over them by the Spirit of the Air. All run to see it, even the small animals (who can be seen at the bottom of the card), because it is necessary to get as near as possible and as quickly as one can to the river of life, once the rainbow quickly disappears.

This Fairy brings new situations and new occassions. One needs to trust in her, even if her offerings and advice may seem uncertain initially. One needs to recognise that the Sylph knows more than the average person. If you are afraid to leave the old for the new, remember that only those who dare will win.

Upright: if you have chosen this card you can consider yourself fortunate. Try to understand the message this Fairy brings to you and use it to the advantage of others and yourself.

Reversed: you have too many sticks in the fire. Abandon those that are uncertain and do not trust promises made in vain. Go with what you feel sure of if you do not wish to loose everything, which is very probable.

THE TROLL – ARCANA XV

The Troll is a negative Fairy, a monster who lives near the barren rocks. All of the Fairies fear him because he does everything he can to trick them and exploit them. He possess a strong magnetism that attracts them, therefore many become his victim. In the classical tarot the Troll corresponds to the Devil, another great tempter.

Be careful therefore of the Troll, disguised in other forms, who is not so difficult to meet in real life.

The Troll dominates the image of this card. He is sitting on a great mound that serves as his throne and at his feet we see a pair of Fairies, his small servants who, fearful of his anger, cannot free themselves from

45

him and blindly follow his evil orders.

The Troll holds a pointed trident in one hand and with the other holds tightly to the chains from which flows the malevolent energy towards the little Fairies. Enormous horns rise from his head and from his wings dangerous claws emerge that try to capture the Fairies who, stupidly, try to pass by.

This Fairy breathes death, fear and disgrace and his every act is a ruinous one, especially for innocent and good spirits. Most of the Fairies are in fact mischevious but basically are not evil.

The XV Arcana is a powerful number, one of high magic, but unfortunately of an evil kind – the so-called black magic – and according to the Bible, corresponds to the great tempter on earth, the Devil. Whoever desires to have lots of money, an important social position, or whatever else without meriting it, sells his soul to the Troll, the Devil, (as the great poet J. Wolfgang von Goethe narrated in his celebrated drama "Faust").

Upright: this card is never a good omen; it warns of a danger about to occur; be very cautious, avoid any changes; be wary of anything you sign.

Reversed: at this time you are not in harmony with yourself; you are short-tempered with everyone and irritated for no reason at all. Have the strength of spirit to wait for this negative influence to pass.

THE TOWER – ARCANA XVI

The Tower represents the pride of the Fairies. It is told that one of their Emperors defied the law of the Kingdom and built a place from stone, declaring it to be indestructable. The superior spirits decided to punish him for his arrogance and made the Tower fall, together with the Emperor. The admonishment for this Fairy was to not believe he was superior to the Creator and to be more humble.

The Tower has four levels: the first floor, without windows, corresponds to mundane knowledge. The first and second floors have one window each, one signifies active action, the other intuitive knowledge. The window on the last floor is that of faith, and is overlooked by a roof of golden hay: it is the divine level.

47

The image of this card is an enormous tower, destroyed by lightning, that has disintegrated the top floor, where a Fairy has dared to be, believing himself to be the same as God, if not greater. The Emperor falls from up high, followed by an enormous stone: only a pile of rubble remains of the magnificent construction. The Fairy however, can see his errors with hindsight, and after a long meditiation, rebuilds and rises up again, but never higher than the Divine One.

The number 16 of the Arcana is of great importance; it is the square root of 4 and expresses all that is tangible, all of the earthly values. The Fairy in fact desired fame and power over the world and over others. Do not forget however that this material number conceals the sacred within it: the sum of 1+6 is 7, the number that is expressed in all the esoteric doctrines

Upright: something very pleasant is about to land unexpectedly upon you, like a gentle rain from the sky, and you will soon realize that this "rain" was necessary to make you happy.

Reversed: you should accept the consequences bestowed upon you and reflect on their meaning as you may well have deserved this run of misfortune. If you are truly sorry and remorseful the lucky 7 will soon bestow joy and new hope upon you.

48

THE NAIAD – ARCANA XVII

A very good fairy, a night spirit who clears the sky of every cloud, thus offering a splendid and luminous sky. The Naiad does everything to free the Fairies of their problems. She also symbolizes nature. This is a card that protects and brings good news. In the classical Tarot it is represented by the Stars; in fact the Naiad's clothes are full of stars that shine brightly in the dark night.

The Fairies see the water nymph in her. The Naiad is smiling blissfully before a lake where she is pouring from two amphor. She pours the waters of life and abundance to fertilize the arid earth and water the vegetation of the forest. Where she walks one can breathe pure air, everything buds with life and awakens the expert to the mysteries hidden within.

49

The Fairies spy on her, hoping to obtain some fortune or a promise, from her. The Naiad however does not like to linger. She flies quickly from one place to another with her splendid double wings. The Fairies go to great lengths therefore to be able to communicate with her, even though they are filled with joy as soon as they see her.

The Fairies consider this Arcana a very lucky number, while humans are divided as to whether the number 17 brings fortune or otherwise. The secret lies in understanding its' dynamic: the numer 17 encloses infinity within it in the number 8, the result of the sum of the two figures 1+7.

Upright: help from higher sources is nearby, therefore if you have a problem, even a very complex one, do not be anxious: the Naiad will find the best solution for you.

Reversed: you find yourself in a difficult situation, or, if not now, you should expect one. Therefore analyze your total situation, both emotional and economic, to avoid trouble. To be victorious depends largely on you.

THE MOON – ARCANA XVIII

The Moon has a strange effect on the Fairies. It causes delusions and errors of the mind during its' various stages. The Moon has such a great influence, especially when full, that it makes the Fairies unpredicatable, with fluctuating moods. They never tire of observing her in her dance across the sky, and remain spellbound by the games the lunar light plays on the vegetation of the forest.

In the card we see two Fairies who look curiously at the full Moon and discuss what she could bestow. It is the moment to ask and to hope that the Moon grants their most intimate wishes. Behind them is a pond, where a lobster is swimming. In fact, the Moon is the Lady of the Zodiac sign of Cancer.

51

This reveals your ability to penetrate your subconscience and to free yourself of the burden of rigid outdated thoughts that have no reason to be there anymore. The Moon however is not as romantic and sweet as she appears. She does not allow you to see things clearly, but brings confusion and frequently unrealizable dreams. This is because she dominates the unconscious which is easy to manipulate emotionally, and reason comes at times too late. The Fairies already have trouble keeping their feet on the ground, and you may also often behave the same.

Upright: you could have a prophetic dream: in this period pay attention to your dreams; your intuition will be accurate. You could also renew an old friendship or a past love.

Reversed: you are in a lazy phase and thus allow important occasions to pass by. Do not wait for miracles; take the reins of your life in hand.

THE MAJOR ARCANA

THE SUN – ARCANA XIX

The Sun is a splendid card in the Fairy Tarot, that will light your path with no clouds in the sky. All situations, either amorous or professional, will appear clear and reassuring.

From bygone days the Sun has been adored, above all by those who have not lost real contact with nature. The Sun has assumed an essential role in all religions: the God Ra in Egypt, Mithra in the Persian religion and Odin in Nordic mythology.

The image of this card is full of a great sun that illuminates everything and renders these gentle folk joyful and carefree. It is the light that can illuminate you, making you realize yours errors, favoured by the deceptive lunar

53

light, and helping you to discern right from wrong and to find the right path. We see a pair of Fairies that dance and laugh in such a way that just by observing the card you may feel as happy as they are. This couple symbolizes the individual spirit, the Ego united with the spirit, therefore the personality of the individual that has attained, with much work, inner harmony and universal love. The wheat that surrounds them is a symbol of richness and abundance, the most valuable seed of growth in every sense.

Above all, the Sun expresses the joy of love, of wanderings and of innocent amusements, but also bestows good health, vitality, positive energy. If there was no Sun in fact, nothing would grow.

Upright: The Sun of the Fairies speaks for itself, and cannot bring anything other than joy and happiness: remember to keep this in mind.

Reversed: the negative side of the Sun is to be blind, to have the tendency to be irritable. If you know how to be calm and are understanding of its' gifts, even if the card is reversed you can hope in the realization of your dreams.

JUDGEMENT – ARCANA XX

This Fairy is the spirit of renewal as it always brings change. It bestows what one deserves; repays with the same currency what one has given or not given. Above all it induces an inner change and judges the morals of each of us, our degree of maturation and urges introspection. This Fairy also carries the role of guardian of the spirits of the dead.

In the card we see an angel of judgement descending from the sky with her trumpet, analogous to the angel Gabriel, which is also mentioned in the Old Testament. The trumpet of the Fairy announces peace and forgiveness on earth; she desires to bring serenity to the world. All of the small sea animals race to hear her call: water in fact expresses the sentiments and the emotions. Not only the acquatic creatures but also those who live in the forest, are attracted to the celestial sounds of her trumpet, which also touch the spirit of the Fairies. This card has good intentions but, according to the situation, also brings punishments, comparable to universal justice: rich in rewards for some, in sufferance for others.

The number 20 expresses the double aspect of the Arcana, composed of the two and the zero. The later as we know, always expresses the universe while the two, duality: the good and the bad, inherent in everything.

Upright: pre-announces a radical inner, spiritual change. You will be more available for others, more understanding and this will bring with it wonderful new friendships and serene interpersonal relationships.

Reversed: all depends on you; an unpleasant piece of news could take you off track, meanwhile if you act in a just manner, with a certain wisdom, what seems negative could in fact turn out to be a future good.

THE WORLD – ARCANA XXI

In the tradition of the Fairies, the world is a unique living entity. If you are able to enter this entity, you will be able to attain perfection and achieve any goal. Even men, when they are happy, say " I could embrace the whole world" unconsciously expressing exactly this living unity.

The image this card presents therefore is a huge globe leaning on the edge of a great rock, while a Fairy, all smiling and sure of himself, attempts to lift it, as if it is his property. He does not have bad intentions but is absolutely convinced that the world is his to play with.

The Fairy, in his great love for nature and for the Creator, can recognize the invisible reality, himself becoming a spirit of the Light. There are no longer

57

secrets, mysteries to discover for the Fairy, who is already part of Everything, of the World.

This Arcana represents the entire creation. You can get all that you desire, above all inner riches and the wisdom that is indespensible for understanding the world and all that is connected to it.

The World however represents also life and the harmony that it maintains with its' laws that must be respected, because if not, chaos would reign. If you have grown spiritually and respect this harmony, you will belong to the World and its gifts. Therefore you can count on the help from this card.

Upright: something very positive is already happening for you, with unexpected joy: you could say " the world is all mine".

Reversed: you desire something that is not in line with the natural laws, something that could damage another person. Make an honest choice, take only that which is your due. This Fairy is a friend to those who are honest with themselves and with others.

THE MEANING OF THE MAJOR ARCANA

O (XXII) – THE ELF: uncertain situation, chaotic; you need to make a difficult decision.
Card upright: protection, resolution within a short time.
Card reversed: resolution but with much effort and reflection.

I – THE MAGICIAN: a winning Fairy, victorious.
Card upright: the Magican will grant your wishes.
Card reversed: success but more time will be needed than imagined.

II – THE HIGH PRIESTESS: the great priestess, an enlightened advisor.
Card upright: you will be blessed by the heavens.
Card reversed: you will see where you have gone wrong, and what you must do.

III – THE EMPRESS: a wise governor, above all regarding your practicality.
Card upright: you can count on her help; she will bestow a sharp mind.
Card reversed: her intelligence, even if you are in difficulty, will know how to get you out of trouble.

IV – THE EMPEROR: he has the spector of command, he is the governor of the earth.
Card upright: creates order and restores justice where it is missing.
Card reversed: he will remove his help if you are not attentive to the social and moral codes.

V – THE HIEROPHANT: the great priest is a wise spiritual guide.
Card upright: you will receive more help and understanding.
Card reversed: if you have faith you can count on him always.

VI – THE LOVERS: this is the card of choice, above all in love.
Card upright: protect your emotional life; marriage is in sight.
Card reversed: problems in love; indicates obstacles from a third party.

VII – THE CHARIOT: success achieved at a gallop.
Card upright: you will clear away any obstacle, especially with regards to love.
Card reversed: you will win, but you must be very patient and understanding.

VIII – THE DRYAD: the spirit of justice, the judge.
Card upright: optimal for legal causes; you will be satisfied with the outcome of controversies.
Card reversed: you risk negative consequences and difficult situations: be careful! 61

IX – THE HERMIT: solitude. the wise one.
Card upright: you need to be introspective, to reflect.
Card reversed: untrusting, pessimistic.

X – THE OREAD: the spirit of fortune.
Card upright: un-hoped for occassions; casually arisen advantages.
Card reversed: fortune will assist you anyway but it is possible you will not realize this immediately.

XI – STRENGTH: a gradual increase in psycho-physical strength.
Card upright: you will develop a strength of spirit that will render you successful wherever: do not fear it.
Card reversed: you are unusually weak; do not take any new initiatives: be careful how you act!

XII – THE HANGED MAN: enclosed within you is an infinite wisdom and sense of responsibility.
Card upright: you must make sacrifices for someone who you love very much; you will be repaid for what you do.
Card reversed: do not be a hero unnecessarily, sacrificing yourself for something that is not worth it: meditate before acting.

XIII – DEATH: the spirit of death that always announces change.
Card upright: fate will make you end something before encountering a better situation.
Card reversed: a sentimental or family breakup most likely a hard experience but try to learn from this.

XIV – THE SYLPH: the spirit who bestows health.
Card upright: regeneration of serenity and happiness.
Card reversed: do not delude yourself too much with a sense of security. Evaluate everything in depth.

XV – THE TROLL: an evil spirit, a terrible monster.
Card upright. A power that could be useful to you but prior to accepting something, be sure of what you will get in return.
Card reversed: the strong magnetism and will of the Troll could drag you into a ditch: faith will help you.

62

XVI – THE TOWER: ruin due to presumptuous ambition.
Card upright: you can build all that you desire, on the condition that you do not feel as if you are God himself.
Card reversed: a hope is fading in your heart, that did not after all have a strong foundation.

XVII – THE NAIAD: a nocturnal spirit.
Card upright: you will be offered a limitless canvas, full of brilliant stars; you will be truly happy.
Card reversed: if a problem worries you, ask for help from this Fairy and all will be set right.

XVIII – THE MOON: emblem of mystery and fascination, emotions, fantasy.
Card upright: rich emotions will render your life beautiful, however do not loose your sense of reality.
Card reversed: someone is trying to fool you, who speaks badly of you: be more cautious in whom you confide.

XIX – THE SUN: luminosity, creativity, fullness.
Card upright: the Sun shines on you in full light; you will fly high in a vortex of joy.
Card reversed: even reversed the Sun shines on you, however remember that it can also burn, especially regarding a passionate affair.

XX – JUDGEMENT: the spirit of renewal.
Card upright: you are put to a test. If you merit it you will be granted serenity and realize your fortune.
Card reversed: for every insincere act or lack of honesty, you may be severely judged.

XXI – THE WORLD: contains everything, riches in every sense, great self-satisfaction.
Card upright. Every door will be open to you, just know which is the most important one for you to knock on.
Card reversed: this Fairy is always a carrier of fortune, perhaps you have a small problem, a choice to make, because there are many occassions and many who love you.

THE SUITES OF MINOR ARCANA

The Suit is defined as a particular symbol of the card, which distinguishes it further from its numerical value or the figure that it represents. In the Tarot system of 78 cards, the 56 Minor Arcana are, along with their Arcana significance, assigned to four suits. The Minor Arcana are divided into 4 groups of 14 cards each, comprised of 10 numbered cards and 4 court cards. Each suit is very important, essential in fact, as it's symbolism assigns it to the group and differentiates one from the other.

According to the suit the card belongs to, the ten numbered cards and the four figures assume a different meaning in the oracle.

In the traditional Tarots the suits are called Cups, Pentacles, Wands and Swords.

In the playing cards however, the so-called French suits are normally used, respectively called: Hearts, Diamonds, Clubs and Spades.

The magic people of the Fairies, creating their own Tarot deck, prefered to use the symbols that corresponded the most with their traditions, habits and customs, related to their close contact with nature. For this reason the four suits in the Fairy Tarot were named Hearts (correspondng to Cups), Bells (corresponding to Pentacles), Acorns (corresponding to Wands) and Leaves (corresponding to Swords).

For the Fairies, as one can easily imagine, the cards of Hearts refer to the world of emotions and sentiments: they talk in particular of affections and of love. They indicate the element of Water.

Any Fairy, when worried about some aspect of a sentimental affair, is more than happy when many favourable cards of Hearts are present in the response.

The suit of Bells however, reveals practical abilities and solutions, the manual capabilities of the Fairies. An inhabitant of that magic kingdom can gain profit from any kind of work. It refers to the element of Earth.

The Bells therefore give the Fairies responses and advice relating to their economic situation and work.

The suit of Acorns is a very important symbol for the Fairy population: in fact in their system of life the acorns constitute a large part of the winter sustainment. They belong to the element of Air.

If a card of Acorns is extracted it means that there is a problem to overcome right now and you must find the strength to resolve it: these cards require a certain patience and focus.

The suit of Leaves is the symbol of thoughts for the Fairy, and thus also, inner existential crisis and contemplation. They refer to the psychic state in general, and are linked to the element of Fire.

Thoughts are similar to clouds carried by the wind: small, grand, white or black and full of rain, they change continually on the backdrop of the sky. No-one knows this changeable state better than the typical Fairy, so carefree but also so sensitive. You also may often feel very much like those small Fairies.

THE ACE OF HEARTS

This is one of the most fortunate cards in the deck. Its image represents a great heart and a lamb, symbols of the good fortune that is given in abundance in all areas and in particular relating to love.

The lamb is smiling, and immediately gives an impression of abundance, of generosity. Its' eyes are reassuring. It is an imortant presence in the magic world of the Fairies, who are often in need of prudent and sensible advice to stop their usual and excessive thoughlessness.

The element of this card is Water, which represents emotions and love above all, of the couple, maternal or of friendship.

The Ace of Hearts symbolizes love and joy in general; the heart that rhythmically pulses within us, a microcosm, in harmony with the rhythm of the entire universe, the macrocosm.

It invites us therefore to have a large heart that encompasses everyone and everthing, and to wish well not only those who are closest to us.

The lamb furthermore advises us to pay attention to the feelings of others and not to play with the hearts of other people.

An upright card promises happiness and abundance; the question that is most important to you will have a satisfactory outcome.

A reversed card indicates some small opposition, perhaps some jealousy or envy, prior to total success.

The writing that appears on the scroll is in Latin and reads: "Curae acuunt mortalia corda". This can be literally translated as "Difficulties make the spirit of mortals stronger". Basically, good comes from bad; troubles make us stronger, and one also needs to learn from one's mistakes.

In the suit of Hearts it needs to be remembered that pain and hurt feelings are at times for our good and they teach us to grow and to advance.

69

TWO OF HEARTS

The Two of Hearts, as the suit suggests, takes us into the realm of the emotions. We see a young man kneeling at the feet of a beautiful young woman who reluctantly turns her head towards him. The image represents an idylic picture, with a fluttering butterfly and a small bird, messengers of news, who appear to be listening to the declarations of love of the young man. To persuade her even more so, he offers her a crown.

All of this represents an unforgetable moment of love, but in reality one must be careful because a person could appear in our lives who seems to be interested in us, but in reality is not. It is only an illusion, as this Fairy fools us!

He is carefree, irresponsible, and does not seriously believe in what he says or promises. For him it is all a game, a joyous and fleeting adventure.

If in the divinatory picture you have drawn this card, you must be more than prudent, as you could find yourself in a situation whereby what appears externally is different to what is underneath. In fact, around the couple are many Fairies who are spying on them and, teasers, are enjoying themselves. If your heart is eager for love, you are more vulnerable and unfortunately, there are less sensitive people in this world than in that of the Fairies.

The number two symbolizes the two principles, apparently opposites, of the male and female, inherent in all things created: without the Sun there would be no Moon; without the night, we would not know day and vice-versa. This polarity is often in conflict, as are humans amongst themselves, instead of harmonizing and complementing each other in turn.

Card upright: excellent! You have managed to avoid the "trap"!

Reversed: you mistake fireflies for lanterns! You are making a blunder!

70

THREE OF HEARTS

This card belongs to the suit of Hearts and logically, makes one consider the emotional world, and love, as it belongs to the element of Water. A magical picture is shown, in which a very small Fairy is portrayed sitting on the ground in the undergrowth and surrounded by birds of different types. It is impossible to give this child a precise age, because the life-span of one who belongs to the magic people of the Fairies can last for centuries.

In his little up-raised hand he holds a small twig, with which he seems to conduct the songs his feathered friends sings.

It is a serene scene that brings to mind a good begining, hope for the future, a promising tomorrow and growth of inner harmony,

The Three of Hearts in fact refers spiritually to inner growth, while on a physical level it represents the evolution of love.

This card, when it appears in your answer, signals a new development for you, progress or an improvement. It announces a happy modification of spirit, the affirmation of your personality. It also could indicate an unexpected notoriety.

Undoubtably this is a promising and timely card. Observe carefully however the totality of the game because if the surrounding cards are negative, nothing will be verified immediately, but only in the near future.

Card upright: triumph or return of love. Realization of hope, and possibly a pregnancy.

Reversed: a prolonged sentimental wait; incubation of an illness with an eventual good outcome.

FOUR OF HEARTS

This card speaks above all to the affective sphere, to the emotions, belonging as it does to the suit of Hearts which is connected to the element of water. What is portrayed is quite problematic however. In fact we see a young Fairy deep in the undergrowth who is holding his arms up in a supplicating manner towards a lovely female contemporary, sitting on a red-capped mushroom.

At the feet of this admirer a precious crown can be seen, overturned, thrown to the ground as if it was an object of no particular value.

What meaning can we give to this scene? Is the young man pleading his sentimental cause or does he have his arms outstretched because the girls has refused his declarations of love?

It is a card that reveals the need for clarity, and to benefit from the inspiration that this moment brings.

Do not be mislead however by the impetus of the heart, even though it is very difficult for anyone to reason objectively in matters of the heart.

It can be concluded that this card advises against inactivity, and against rash acts, which certainly could severely embarass the Fairies, always impulsive and hasty, as perhaps some of us are too.

Card upright: transient love, new sentimental occurrences; a choice that weighs heavily on one's heart.

Reversed: troubled spirit, some remorse, possibility of separation, divorce.

FIVE OF HEARTS

The appearance of this card in the suit indicates that reference is being made to the emotional sphere, to love, linked to the element of water. The image offered is that of an attractive young girl from the magical people of the Fairies, curled up on the head of a giant mushroom in the forest. At the foot of this makeshift throne we see a young male Fairy.

This heartsick lover, having seranaded the girl, has placed his mandolin on the ground and has taken into his hands a lock of her hair to kiss it.

The girl is pleased but a little shy, even if she doesn't want him to see this. In fact she watches him through the fingers of her hands which she has placed over her face.

This is a delicate picture, even if it leaves one a little perplexed. Will the adoration of this Fairy last for long, knowing his natural disposition is restless and fickle?

The Five of Hearts, if it appears in your oracle, indicates you are experiencing a moment of stagnation that could preceed a new development.

It is a card therefore that advises reflection and prudence in matters of love, judgement in the choice of friends. It alerts you to be on guard for dangerous relationships that could bring displeasures and losses.

It could allude to a possible marriage: accompanied by other favourable cards and this union could be advantageous from an economic viewpoint. If accompanied by unfavourable cards, it simply means a marriage, neither good nor bad.

73

SIX OF HEARTS

The beautiful leaves that can be seen in the background of this card appear to belong to a species that grows near water, in perfect harmony with its suit of Hearts, which refer to this element, to the emotions and to love.

In the shadows of this vegetation we note a Fairy who is bending towards his loved one to kiss her, while the little Fairies fly above them with an expression that is both curious and cheeky, but also a little shy for having disturbed them. It is a sweet magical moment, one that remains imprinted on the memory and that one evokes willingly in moments of sadness or worry.

The Fairies have many small and great joys, but they, like everyone else, also have regrets and sorrows, that happy memories can possibly allieviate.

If you have chosen this card in your oracle, it is significant in some way in your present or future.

The Six of Hearts does not imply difficult choices for you but rather brings hesitiations and insecurity due to fear of making a mistake. It could also encourage you to have patience, to appease impatience or sorrows and to think about lovely times passed.

It could therefore also indicate having scruples, regarding a decision to be taken concerning a marriage or a union.

Card upright: hesitations of the heart; bitter-sweet memories.

Reversed: separation, pangs of love.

THE SUITES OF MINOR ARCANA

SEVEN OF HEARTS

In this image we see a Fairy riding on the back of a huge green frog. He is near a pond in the middle of the water-lillies, that return us to the element of Water and to the suit of Hearts.

The Fairy has a hood made from an upturned flower on his head, and on his back, a petal makes him a cape. He observes, engrossed, the apparation of a small winged creature, that seems to rise from the water.

Undoubtably what he sees is only a vision, judging from the contrast between the presence of this Fairy, which is crystal clear and linked to reality, and the diaphanous, ethereal vision of this apparition.

The Fairies are a magical people and they are sensitive and intuitive. They often have visions and premonitory dreams, to which they pay a lot of attention. We however tend not to, and slowly but surely, we are loosing contact with other planes of existence, more subtle than the world that surrounds us.

Attention therefore is needed if this card appears in your response. Do not be sceptical or connected only to the appearances of concrete reality. Follow the example of the Fairies and let sensitivity, intuition (those faculties also called intelligence of the heart) to allow you to gather every sign, every warning that you can.

The Seven of Hearts can also indicate the existence in your mind of projects, that the remaining cards in the reading should make clear as to what they refer .

Card upright: forebodings, premonitory dreams; situations developing. You could encounter a person to truly love.

Reversed: luck in love after a struggle; unpleasant passions that could win.

EIGHT OF HEARTS

The card carries the suit of Hearts, therefore it is evident it refers to the element of Water and to the world of emotions, sentiments and to love.

Pictured is a glade in the woods, where grass and mushrooms grow. In this place, quiet and protected, some Fairies are happily enjoying themselves, playing and jumping over a little rodent, their friend.

We immediately see that these magical creatures feel very much at ease, in contact with nature –which is very important for them- and is probably the most concrete link they feel (given their carefree and roaming character). It could give them a solid and stable point of reference.

This is an inspiring picture, in the serenity and the obvious harmony between the Fairies and the surrounding nature. It talks of peace, of equilibrium and harmony. An equilibrium so natural and spontaneous exists in that magic Kingdom, while we in our world vex ourselves looking for it desperately, alas, without ever finding it.

It is good if this card appears in your oracle, as it reveals that you are in a harmonious moment. There is an equilibrium between the emotions, passions and reason and your spiritual components.

The Eight of Hearts also indicates that there is a change coming for you, a new situation, that could develop very positively.

Card upright. Reciprocated love, harmony in love.

Reversed: incompatable characters; prohibited love.

NINE OF HEARTS

In this card, in the middle of the grass in the undergrowth, a huge mushroom arises, with its' red hat. On it is seated a little fairy, who has on her back a cape made from the petals of a flower.

What is she doing there, all alone, this creature who loves to laugh and joke with the other Fairies so much?

Even if they are carefree and playful, every now and then a Fairy will remove himself/herself from the company of his/her companions in order to meditate alone. She/He needs to gather inspiriation, serenity and peace by complete contact with nature, which surrounds him/her and which she/he loves so much.

This card carries the suit of hearts, belonging to the element of Water, therefore it addresses the world of emotions and sentiments. If it appears in your oracle then you can be satisfied.

It is in fact a happy card that brings joy and calm. It also indicates physical wellbeing, consolidated projects or favourable events in the future.

It could indicate that momentary pause prior to a departure or an initiative. The nine of Hearts however also advises meditation in solitude and reflection, which are indispensible to find oneself again, above all in our chaotic days, exactly as the image of this Fairy in meditation suggests.

Card upright: favourable for a complete union, physical and sentimental; respect for the traditions of the family and of principles.

Reversed: an unusual or cerebral love affair; a union with an older person.

77

TEN OF HEARTS

A truly lovely picture, what we see represented in this card!

There is hardly any need of the suit of Hearts to understand that this card refers to the emotional and sentimental sphere, to the element of Water.

Observing the card in fact we can see a multitude of tiny Fairies stretched out in a glade in the woods, under the yellow umbrella of an enormous mushroom, having a peaceful siesta together in the shade.

It is clear that they belong to a peaceful people, and are all friends who care about each other and are ready to help each other in harmony.

Have you extracted this card in your response?

It is good luck for you, a positive symbol that reveals all that love and friendship can include, or imply. It talks of harmony and understanding, affections and relationships with other people.

The ten of Hearts in your consultation can signify a happy conclusion, a final stage reached at the right moment, as this reunion of Fairies demonstrates. They are in agreement about their objective – the desire to have a peaceful rest together.

Card upright: happy sentimental change; numerous friends; harmony, understanding in love.

Reversed: sentimental disharmony, distancing from friends, obstacles to a conclusion.

THE KNAVE OF HEARTS

The Fairy that appears in this card seems to be very proud, adorned with a type of brown uniform and a long mustard-coloured jacket. He wears a red beret on his head, the top point of which is truncated with a red stone in the shape of a heart at the centre of the folded brim.

The large and rounded buckle of his belt, almost a small shield, holds a formidable sword, also adorned with a red heart in the centre.

The reference to the the element of Water, to the emotive and affective world of the suit of Hearts is more than clear, confirmed by these two ornamental hearts.

Our Fairy holds a crossbow firmly on his back with one hand, and thus armed, has a self-confident air with an open and sincere expression that inspires trust and confidence.

When the Fairies in their magic Kingdom consult the Tarot for resolving a question or for some wise advice, this card represents a young good-looking man, who has brilliant ideas and who could be a good friend.

If you are still young and this card appears in your response, this Knave could be a representation of yourself. In general however it relates to a promising youth, a student or a person who is about to begin an activity.

The Knave of Hearts can also indicate an adolescent overcome by the first feelings of love, or the first phase –perhaps a little conflictual – of a union. Card upright: tendency towards sentimentality; passionate love even if unfaithful, but without malice, love for a younger person.

Reversed: unlucky in love; betrayal of friends.

THE KNIGHT OF HEARTS

This card presents us with the image of a Knight belonging to the Fairy people. The animal that he rides is not a horse but rather a powerful turtle.

This Fairy wears the army uniform of his magical Kingdom, with the brim of his hat decorated with a red heart-shaped stone, as is the buckle that holds the sword. In his right hand he holds a halberd, while with his left he guides his "stead".

The suit of Hearts refers to the element of Water, and to the affective and emotional sphere.

The Knight Fairy has an expression of self-confidence and of pride. Even if his smiling face tells you he is good and generous and ready to help, he is hard on his adversaries, though he is gentle with his friends.

It could easily be infered that this Fairy arrives from far-away and that he brings good news, given his friendly face. Perhaps he brings gifts or tempting proposals. It is a good sign if this card appears in your response. It indicates a man free of sentimental attachments, a bachelor and independent, experienced in the world.

This card indicates success in matters of the heart, or that happiness is on its way.

Card upright: loving transformation, triumphal renewal of an old love; good news.

Reversed: a rival in love; a seducer, news that is not good.

80

THE QUEEN OF HEARTS

The figure that we see in this card is immediately likeable. In fact the aspect of this Queen is regal in terms of her clothing but her expression is kind-hearted and sweet. One can imagine her great sensitivity and her generous goodness.

This Queen of the Fairies wears a magnificent dress of pale lilac, decorated around the hem with little hearts, while on her back she carries a long red cape. She has long wavy hair, and is standing on a green carpet. On her head she wears a precious gem-studded crown and she hold a spectre in her hands, the point adorned with a red heart.

The small hearts on her clothing, the heart on the spectre and the suit of Hearts all allude to the element of Water and therefore to love, the emotions and sentiments.

In the Tarot of the Fairies this Queen is the symbol of kindness, of spiritual sensitivity. Furthermore it indicates a loyal and good friend; the same Fairy that they consult.

If you have extracted this card, consider it to be positive, as it refers to a person who is a friend and who is sincere; a mother, a woman who will suffer more for others than for herself, who is happy or unhappy depending on the moods of those around her. If you are a woman and are verifying your own response, it can also indicate yourself.

Card upright: an intelligent woman, honest: a woman who will sacrifice herself for love; a friend who protects you.

Reversed: a treacherous woman, to be feared; a trap from a female; a rival in love.

THE KING OF HEARTS

In this card we see a Fairy seated on a throne that is placed over a green carpet laid over the earth of the forest. This Fairy is a King. He has a majestic air and makes one feel a little uneasy. He is wearing a red gown with the sleeves edged in white fur. His surcoat is of pale lilac and is hemmed with many small hearts. He wears a precious gold crown and his right hand leans on the red heart at the top of the spectre, the emblem of his power.

The suit of Hearts of this card refers to the element of Water as do the ornamental hearts: they all speak of love, the emotions and the sentiments.

The flowing beard and the long white whiskers of the Fairy King show him to be an elderly person, while his heightened colour makes one think he is quite hot-tempered. But one can imagine his temper is short-lived, more to admonish and correct than to punish.

It is known that the Fairies are generally restless and cheeky and do not like authority much, but this King represents for them a sure reference point, and a symbol of stability and maturity that even they at some point in their long lives, desire to have.

If the King of Hearts appears in your response, it is easy to deduce that it indicates an elderly man, almost always married, perhaps representing your father. But it could also symbolize a man of the law, always however, a person who is intelligent, cultured, virtuous, who could advise you well; a person of deeds rather than empty words.

Card upright: stability in love; the support of a man of some standing
Reversed: immature love; a dissolute or effeminate man.

ACE OF BELLS

This card shows a white rabbit dressed in a stiff white collar and a blue hat, from which emerge his long ears.

He has a captivating apppearance that inspires trust and sympathy, but he appears rather serious and decisive as if he is hurrying to some important appointment.

We need not be fooled into judging this serious and busy creature, because in the Kingdom of the Fairies the suit of Bells, which appears on this card, is the symbol of work, of craftsmanship. It refers to the element of Earth, to the sphere of buisness and professional capabilities.

It is not by chance however that the symbol for work, money and for

richness is for the Fairies united in a gentle rabbit, seemingly undefended. In their work world earning money does not necessarily imply the overpowering of others but must always be characterised by loyalty and honesty.

The Ace of Bells therefore talks of fortune, power and of happiness. If this card appears first in your divination, you could even stop here, as it indicates how much better things will be. When it appears along with negative cards, it announces that every obstacle will be overcome, each contrary event dominated.

Card upright: inheritance, victory, advantageous work contract, professional realization.

Reversed: do not be discouraged, the answer is always positive. What is promised will not be verified immediately but in the near future.

The writing that appears on the scroll is in Latin and reads: "Discipulus est prioris posterior dies". This can be translated directly as "He who is a disciple will be a master tomorrow". This is a recall to time, to the just sequence of things and the gradual nature of growth. Just as the disciple will be the master, the master was also once a disciple.

83

TWO OF BELLS

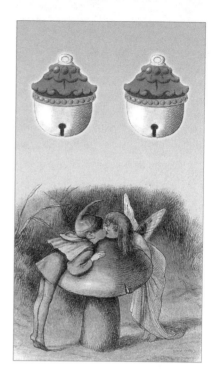

The image portrayed here is of a glade in the forest with a large mushroom. A Fairy wearing a red pointed beret leaning over the red top of the mushroom is kissing a lovely young girl, also one of the enchanted people.

This picture could easily be entitled: "Idyll in the forest", as it is so enchanting!

Observing closely however, it can be seen that it is the suit of Bells that identify this card and we know they refer to the element of Earth and to the world of work and buisness. This little scene therefore, even if delicate, is in its entirety rather out of place and altogether in the wrong context.

The young Fairy therefore is a little absent-minded, a little unaware. He is not intending to do any harm but is obviously neglecting his work and obligations to instead court his beloved. This clearly is not a negative card if it appears in your oracle. In fact together with other positive cards, it could refer to small annoyances getting in the way of favourable events.

It could also announce the arrival of a letter or a telephone call, that could alert you to something important.

Card upright: delay of a project or a payment or the conclusion of a transaction.

Reversed: small troubles coming; advice against gambling or placing bets of any type.

THREE OF BELLS

The group of Fairies, composed of boys and girls, that can be seen in this card, are very much caught up in a rather particular game. One of these Fairies in fact tries to hold onto a butterfly by the tip of its' wings while the others observe him intently.

The curiosity of the Fairy people is proverbial. They are easily distracted by any little thing, let alone the arrival of a such a large and beautiful butterfly!

Consulting their Tarot, the Fairies know that when this card appears with its suit of Bells, it refers to the element of Earth and to the sphere of work and buisness and therefore they expect to shortly meet someone famous or important or a person who may be very useful to know.

The three of Bells also has this meaning in your oracle: it indicates celebrity, considerations, a profitable and close at hand transformation of buisness affairs and in general; the favourable transformation of a situation.

This card is positive and reveals that, if the events preannounced by the divination should be negative, it will only be because of something the person consulting the cards has not done. Make sure it is not you!

Card upright: well-conducted buisness affairs; money on the way; a win at gambling; meeting an important person.

Reversed: be careful not to be tempted to trick someone else and harm them: it will turn against you!

FOUR OF BELLS

This card contains a rather particular scene, other than the four of Bells that refers to the element of Earth, the area of work and of buisness.

In the grass of this undergrowth we see a huge mushroom with a red top, on which a Fairy with a funny red beret is perched. He observes somewhat enviously one of his companions stretched out at the foot of the mushroom in the shade. This Fairy, who seems to be an important person with his red cloak and a golden crown on his head, is enjoying a wonderful nap, while a large scarab, a symbol of fortune and richess, moves nearby.

In the magical world of the Fairies success in an activity undertaken is important, not only because it brings material benefits but also equilibrium and inner strength, the stability that they aim for given their restless nature. The card relays all of this with the image of the Fairy sleeping serenely due to the tranquility conferred by the pre-eminent position gained, and by the charmed scarab.

It is a favourable card in your response. It announces fortune, inheritance , gifts, gratifications. If the other cards are by chance negative, you must pay attention to your behaviour. Even a small disagreement or an ordinary incident could have unfavourable consequences.

Card Upright: fortune, an increase in salary; financial ordering, gifts.

Reversed: an expected gift that you must however take in another form; joy that comes at a high price.

86

FIVE OF BELLS

The image that this card presents places us in front of a rather disconcerting scene. Between the branches of a tree is a large nest containing an egg while a big bird with a yellow beak is perched on the edge. The bird has an expression that seems both surprised and angry. He seems uncertain of what to do next. He can't be blamed however, as we can see nearby a Fairy who is running away, his red cape flying, with an egg in his arms, evidently just taken from the nest when the bird was away searching for food.

The Fairies are generally cheeky, but happy and carefree, playing tricks thoughtlessly perhaps but not to be unkind. Unfortunately some of them are greedy and don't think twice before taking whatever they want in whatever manner possible.

This card, with its suit of Bells that refers to the world of work, buisness and the element of Earth, appears in your oracle to place you on guard. It warns against greed, avarice, and, by implication, even desiring something you cannot afford, or aiming too ambitiously.

To take strides that are too big for your legs is always a source of trouble and unhappiness.

Card upright: a person or an event that you cannot defend yourself against; the possibility of setbacks; a disorderly life.

Reversed: you are too ambitious: be careful of false moves, you could trip yourself up.

SIX OF BELLS

This card illustrates a most romantic moment: between the leaves of a branch are some rose buds. One, large and beautiful of an intense pink color has just bloomed.

A Fairy, splendidly dressed in a red tunic and a beret decorated with two long soft curved plumes, embraces another lovely Fairy. She is seated on the flowering rose and gently rests her head on the arms of her companion. A graceful two-toned butterfly flutters nearby.

This card has a very positive significance for the Fairies when it appears in their consultation of the Tarot, as it indicates solidarity, an important value for a people who are united and affectionate amongst themselves.

If you have extracted the six of Bells, whose suit refers to the element of Earth and to the sphere of work and buisness, you can expect help, either given or received, in an opportune moment; an awaited acceptance or a promotion long hoped for. If you are still umarried, it could indicate a person of some social standing is interested in you.

Card Upright: make good use of the money you earn; un-hoped for earnings; an increase in your buisness affairs.

Reversed: momentary trouble with money; loss of money due to bad advice.

88

SEVEN OF BELLS

The image on this card shows a branch covered with leaves, with a large red flower, a trumpet-like-flower, at the top.

Seated near the beautiful flower on a leaf, is a child-like Fairy, with his arms open, laughing at a large splendid butterfly that has rested on another leaf in front of him.

There is a wonderful harmony, an ideal matching between the little Fairy, the flower and the butterfly.

It is in fact known that the Fairies have a great love of the woods and for all the creatures in their magic al Kingdom. They respect and care for the nature surrounding them, which repays them by always giving them everything they need.

With the suit of Bells, this card refers to the element of Earth, the area of work, buisness and of earnings. The appearance of this card is a very positive sign. It indicates benefits gained through one's work and intelligence.

Conscientiousness, constant effort and moral strength, will always bring results in any activity. It could also indicate that there will soon be new interests in the intellectual arena.

Card upright: you will be helped by money, or will benefit from an advantageous transaction.

Reversed: generosity, from which you receive and also share.

EIGHT OF BELLS

This card represents a moment in the daily life of the Fairies who do not always pass their time joking and having fun but who will, for their beloved creatures of the woods, endeavour to do their best.

We can see two Fairies close to a lovely small animal that has a long thick tail, probably a squirrel. One of them is holding its front leg in his hand while the other is sitting on its tail to keep it from moving. It is easy to deduce that this little rodent has hurt itself and the Fairies are trying to help it.

A third smaller Fairy however is attempting to free a multicoloured butterfly from something it has entangled itself in. Another white butterfly observes them from above.

In the Tarot of the Fairies, the eight of Bells (the suit of which refers to the world of work and earnings) indicates the activities they are involved in, for example helping the creatures of the forest, and their professional and enterprenurial capacities.

This is a favourable card to appear in your response. It reveals many positive moments in your activities, a timely renewal of situations that were uncetain and that now become clear. It could also signify a just distribution of goods.

Card upright: there could be a verification of a positive change in your work, an uncontested inheritance.

Reversed: preoccupations regarding the work that you do; a contested inheritance, of goods unjustly distributed.

90

NINE OF BELLS

The scene presented in this card is very lovely and joyous. It shows an incoronation in the magic woods of the Fairies. We can see some of the Fairies seated on leaves and branches, surrounded by many small winged creatures of diverse species, perched also on the branches.

One of these Fairies is placing a gold crown on the head of a beautiful bird, chubby and round, but seemingly serious and composed, wearing a regal red mantle with a collar of white fur.

This ceremony represents a very important moment in the life of the Kingdom of the Fairies, as it confirms a success acheived, seen in the eyes of everyone, an affirmation that merits recognition.

The suit of the nine of Bells belongs to the element of Earth, and refers to the area of work and buisness. Therefore if it appears in your response it is a positive sign for you as it signifies that your work activities, your abilities in that area, will or are about to obtain the desired success and recognition from others.

You can consider this card favourable even if you have new projects to begin or new initiatives. It could also pre-announce some luck or fortune coming from the work area; perhaps gifts, perhaps some discovery.

Card upright: improvised movement of money; change or travel for work, study, that could combine work with pleasure.

Reversed: a missed success; some obstacle or delay in the realization of a project.

TEN OF BELLS

In the middle of beautiful brightly blossoming flowers, we see a Fairy with a baby (most probably hers) in her arms. The baby is wearing a beret and a small cape, both red and brand new. Near her is another small Fairy trying to put on a shoe. A little further away from this group a kind Fairy is kneeling to tie a red cape around the neck of a third child.

This scene refers to a very generous and lovely custom of the magical Fairy people: whoever amongst them receives an inheritance, something relatively important, never hesitates to share at least some part of this with the others. They are carefree these Fairies and thoughtless but they have a heart that could be said to be greater than them!

The ten of Bells refers to the area of work and money and to the element of Earth. When this card appears therefore, it means money is on the way for you. It could indicate an inheritance or a donation or even the discovery of a treasure or else a sudden increase in one's patrimony.

You are advised therefore to follow the good customs of the Fairies and to enable others to participate in your fortune, with the spontaneity and the sincere feeling that those magic creatures have.

Card upright: remarkable earnings; increase in goods; concrete acknowledgments.

Reversed: large loss of money in general, even at gambling; a contested inheritance.

92

KNAVE OF BELLS

At the back of the undergrowth, with the plants full of flowers and fruit, is a Fairy standing firmly on the ground. He has a decisive air about him. He is sure of himself, with his lovely green outfit complete with his leather justicoat and a sword strap over his shoulder. His head is covered with a type of helmet without a brim, also made of leather. He holds in his hand a robust handle of a shiny dark colour, which he leans on.

To better understand this person we need to observe that the suit of this card, being Bells, refers to the element of Earth and to the work area, buisness and artisan capabilities.

This card for the Fairies indicates a young person with innovative ideas, but one who removes himself a little from traditional methods. Therefore they can admire him, but always maintain a little reserve.

This card appearing in your response therefore indicates a young person who proposes something regarding work. It could be a colleague in the office, a friend, someone you should listen to objectively, without being immediately convinced by his reasoning. It could be interesting or could, umwillingly lead you to trouble. At times genial discoveries can end up being disastarous for those who put them into practice.

Card upright: a likeable youth, but not to be depended on; bad investment of money.

Reversed: it is good to remember the old saying: " Those who leave the old for the new...." with the consequences to be reckoned with.

KNIGHT OF BELLS

This card from the suit of Bells, which refers to the world of work and buisness, connected to the element of Earth, shows between the flowering grasses of the woods, a proud Fairy riding on the back of a splendid red squirrel, with a large thick tail.

This Knight holds in his left hand the reins of his mount and with his right hand holds a lance. He has a helmet on his head. It can be seen that he is used to long voyages by his practical and light clothing, and by the comfortable and soft shoes he wears on his feet. His expression is kind, even if his face, a smile just fading on it, is one of someone who has lived and experienced things he cannot discuss.

In the many travels that must be undertaken when carrying out an assignment, the Fairies get to know many people, other customs and traditions and can have great experiences. This Knight is therefore listened to and often consulted for his good and well mediated advice (fruit of the life he has lived).

When this card appears in your oracle, it suggests that you must gain the assistance of an expert person. Advice will not be enough, even objective advice and that given in good faith by a relative or a friend. You need help from someone with experience in the area that concerns you.

Card upright: relationships that bear good fruit; a new, useful friendship; the arrival of money by post.

Reversed: it is not always true that what is good for a penny is good for a pound...better to spend a little more rather than make a mess of things.

94

QUEEN OF BELLS

The Queen of Bells that we see in this card has a real air of triumph and prosperity. The suit refers precisely to money, riches, work and all that is relevant to the element of Earth.

The laughing Fairy seated on a throne situated amongst the grasses of the woods, wears a beautiful green surcoat over a white tunic decorated with many tiny gold bell-flowers.

This Queen has a splendid ornate gold crown on her head, and in her white-gloved left hand she holds a pole with a type of curved spectre from which hangs a small bell, once again of gold.

Everything in this card speaks of riches and well-being. Her smile is fresh and spontaneous, that of a person who is vivacious and active and who enjoys what she possess and wishes others to also participate.

It symbolizes well the generous nature of the Fairies, who are spontaneous and altruistic even if they are kissed by fortune, covered in riches or at the apex of succes.

In your oracle this card signifies generosity, or a woman, perhaps independently wealthy, who can assist you in practical terms. It also reveals the ability to know how to use a good position. If you are a woman it announces fortune.

Card upright: expect gifts from rich relatives; or money lent by a woman, if needed.

Reversed: you have richness but you are unhappy emotionally; possibility of boredom in the family, or with your activity, caused by women.

KING OF BELLS

On his high throne of painted wood, in the middle of the grass and flowers of the woods, a Fairy is seated. He has a serious and determined air, and rests both his hands on the hilt of a sword, the tip of which rests on the earth.

He is wearing sumptuous clothing: from the green tunic under a white vest embroidered with many tiny gold bells and the soft suede leather shoes, to the crown that decorates his beret with a pure gold bell at the top. One can see that this Fairy is a very wealthy and powerful person. The suit of Bells of this card refer to the element of Earth, to money, to work and buisness.

This Fairy symbolizes a person who has reached the apex of his activity and through his own work and intelligence, has earned great wealth and possessions, and is therefore a king over his own land.

The Fairies, if they apply themselves seriously, can attain very important economic positions.

This card in your response indicates a man of a certain age, married: an industrialist or a rich merchant, a banker, a property owner or a person who is wealthy and esteemed but egotisical –one whom it is better to be friends with and not enemies.

Card upright: announcement of a marriage that is more advantageous than sentimental; a person who could offer you a lucrative buisness opportunity.

Reversed: a rich man who could help you for his own interests: unhappiness due to a union out of self-interest; a rich man, very materialistic.

ACE OF LEAVES

The Ace of Leaves is one of the most important and significant cards that can be found in the Tarot of the Fairies. It guarantees the maximum success in whatever area you wish for.

The suit of Leaves that distinguishes it, is the symbol of thoughts and of intellectual abilities. It therefore also regards existential crisis, to which we are all easily subjected .

The image of this card is very appealing. At the center of the card we see a great porcupine, whose back legs are resting on a large leaf, which partly covers it. Only it's snout can be seen well. Another green leaf is resting on its head.

The expression of this animal is very sweet. He observes with his

large engrossed eyes all that is happening around him and seems to be thinking of how he can be of assistance to his people.

It is a good sign if this card appears in your oracle. If you have some important wish in any sector of your life, you will fully realize it, but only if you apply yourself seriously. This porcupine of the Fairies is not generous to those who do not commit themselves totally, therefore he can be of assistance but you must work hard, if this applies to your profession.

Card upright: you can be sure that fortune is on your side

Reversed: put more enthusiasm and positive thought into achieving your aims, otherwise they will remain a mirage.

The writing that apears on the scroll is in Latin and reads: "Assem habeas assem valeas". This can be literally translated as "You are worth what you have", but its' real significance as a motto is in fact: You are worth the things you are able to do and attain. In reality this is an incentive to substance rather than superficiality; deeds rather than words. The "value" refered to in the original Latin motto was an economic and monetary value, but for the Leaves suit of the Faires, this is transformed – as is the " have" – into a metaphoric meaning.

TWO OF LEAVES

The picture on this card shows two leaves up high and a nest well-hidden between the leafy branches of a tree, occupied by a bird and its' clutch. We see two small birds trying to hide behind their mother's head, who is trying with her beak to keep another one from being taken from the nest by a cheeky Fairy. This Fairy doesn't really want to take the little chick from its mother, but it is a little proud and vain and wants to show his skill and his bravery, in a difficult endeavour that requires courage.

The two Leaves indicate the constant search for equilibrium between the adversities of life, that this Fairy knows very well how to overcome as he is bold and knows how to adapt to unexpected situations. It also represents a union, but also the opposition that one needs to understand and therefore complement.

If you have chosen this card, you can count on solidarity. This card inevitably announces a friend. Only courageous and moral people, as the Fairy demonstrates, can be of assistance and support.

You will have diverse help in projects, or in questions of the heart especially from friends, if you speak openly and sincerely with them.

This is always a positive card, even reversed. In this case however the Fairy succeeds in assisting you but with some effort; you need patience as it could be that in this moment you do not know how to ask, talk or deal with things in the right way.

Card upright: if you have need of something, ask without fear.

Reversed: put pride aside, as it will do you no good. A smile, a handshake, will bring you much more.

THE SUITES OF MINOR ARCANA

THREE OF LEAVES

The Three of Leaves is not a good omen. It is a card that brings sad announcements. Observing the picture it can be seen immediately that future events will not be positive. We see in fact a young Fairy under mushroom, crying quietly, covering his face with both hands,while one of his companions flies off, away from him.

It is a picture of abandonment and there is nothing to be seen here that could give one hope of a change for the better. The three Leaves above, other than giving a numerical value to the card, refers to the world of thoughts and of existential crisis.

This is a card that is feared by the magical Fairy people, as all know that its appearance is not auspicious. Unfortunately it cannot be avoided and one cannot flee from painful events, which are all part of life. Frequently however, after some time, what was a huge sorrow can turn out to be for the best.

If this card has appeared in your response, try to understand and to accept: remember that the sun always shines after a storm!

This card, even upright, is never a good omen; the only positive indicator is that whatever the problem is or the sorrow you are dealing with, you will overcome it with courage and in a balanced manner. The event will be for you over time an experience that has taught you much, even if right now that seems impossible.

Card upright: you could experience an emotional misfortune, following which your heart remains broken for some time: it will seem that the whole world is crumbling around you.

Reversed: it has the same significance as the upright card.

FOUR OF LEAVES

The four of Leaves has an image that is not serene. A Fairy is seated alone in a nest, where he is hoping to be left in peace, lost in his own sad thoughts. Four birds however are trying to peck at him with their beaks to make him leave, while he protects himself with his hands.

The Fairy has looked for an isolated place to reflect and to think calmly, but there is always someone who doesn't want to leave him alone. He is, unusually, a thinker, and many of his companions do not understand him.

The four of Leaves is a card of solitude, demonstrated by the Fairy who does not connect with the other Fairies. Their thoughtlessness and desire to joke all the time annoys him.

At the top we see the four Leaves which convey the numerical value of the card and that by their suit indicate the sphere of the mind.

This card always indicates a certain solitude, moments of melancholy. It awakens one to the fact that at this time you need to draw back a little into yourself, to reflect on various situations in order to make some decisions, and you need to do this without asking for advice from others.

The pre-announced solitude of the card is not what you have wished for but you are obliged to accept it, because someone has left you alone.

You must slowly but surely realize that nothing happens by chance and that destiny will lead you to other objectives.

Card upright: you are immersed in sad thoughts, and even if someone attempts to make you smile, they will not succeed.

Reversed: there is someone near to you who wishes to interfere: you must not allow this!

100

FIVE OF LEAVES

This card shows three Fairies, two of whom are holding onto the leg of a dragonfly to stop it from flying away while the third Fairy, who has fallen over, pushes his leg against the nearest Fairy's back to help him hold onto their prey.

The picture we see expresses the will to destroy, to not consider the feelings of others. These three Fairies are even more disruptive than their companions. They risk loosing things or they destroy them, and undo what should remain united.

At the top there is the numerical indication expressed by the five Leaves, the suit that refers to the mind, the psyche.

The five of Leaves is considered by the Fairies to be a rather negative card. It indicates someone with little conscience, who does not manage or want to maintain interpersonal relationships and who has many superficial acquaintances.

This card therefore is unfavourable even in your oracle, as it indicates unmotivated violence, the will to harm, more or less consciously, in order to remove a sorrow or a hurt that is in your heart and mind. You act on impulse, demonstrating a certain egocentricity that you do not really possess in your heart.

Card upright: you cannot overcome an existential crisis by making others suffer. You are acting unjustly to those who love you and who wish for your happiness.

Reversed: negative tendencies are reinforced, as there is neither the will nor the depth to analyse oneself, to try and understand the true motive for this wrong behaviour.

SIX OF LEAVES

The picture on this card illustrates a pond with lots of vegetation around it, where we see a large acquatic bird being ridden by a Fairy, and another concealed by a waterlily a little further away. Below, a fish gasps in amazement, while above another bird hovers, perplexed as to the unusual means of locomotion.

It is known that all Fairies fly, but at times they prefer to get about by other rather strange means. With a thirst for even stronger emotions, new experiences, they love to dream and hope that one of them will in fact realize his dreams. This card therefore is a good omen for their wishes. Who amongst us does not have a secret dream that one day we hope will come true?

The Fairies do not have constant thoughts however. They take life as it comes and if they cannot fly they immediately contrive of some means to overcome the obstacle, as the Fairy in this card illustrates.

If you have extracted this card you can be sure that something good and unusual is on the way: a trip that you dared not hope for; a meaningful experience; or else you will devise an intelligent means of resolving a situation. On the negative side, this card reveals that you could receive great promises that are not maintained. Therefore do not loose yourself in unrealisable dreams and do not blindly trust persuasive words.

Card upright: news in arrival, perhaps strange, rare or unexpected; a successful device.

Reversed: you can count on some good news in just the right measure, or on an unexpected joy.

SEVEN OF LEAVES

This card shows a Fairy on the back of a leafy branch, with two birds flying nearby. This Fairy, with his red beret decorated with a long feather, seems intent on explaining something to the bird in front of him, which is listening with a very serious expression.

Higher up there are the seven Leaves, which, other than giving the numerical value of the card, refer to the mind. This is an entertaining scene, but it is one of the customs of the inhabitants of this magic Kingdom to solicit advice from diverse sectors for projects they have in mind, therefore there really is little to marvel about. It could possibly be that this Fairy is concluding an important transaction with the inhabitants of the woods...

It is good to listen to the opinions of others regarding one's ideas as the Fairies do, as long as you do not become confused by their opinions which, from lack of all the information or from incomprehension, could perhaps lead you astray.

This card therefore indicates projects and transactions, but also appointments and interviews, which could be close at hand. It could also refer to a marriage, if it appears in your response next to a card of Hearts.

Card upright: you will positively realize all that you have undertaken to do; beneficial or interesting contacts.

Reversed: unfruitful transactions; inconclusive chatter, discussions.

EIGHT OF LEAVES

This card has a picture that is a little veiled and sombre. We see bare branches with Fairies resting on them. There is also a small animal in the middle of them. In front of them is a Fairy lying on the ground in an immobile state, which is in great contrast to her innate vitality. The scene lacks the animation and the vivacity that normally distinguishes life in the magic Kingdom, and this change clearly indicates a concern. It could be an illness in the incubation phase, or an inner crisis. The suit of Leaves in fact indicates that this card refers to the sphere of the mind, of the psyche.

When the Fairies extract the eight of Leaves in their response, they know well that this is a warning, that it could perhaps announce a radical change of life.

If this card appears in your oracle, you are probably experiencing a lull in some sector of your life and you are unsure of what to do. You are experiencing an inner crisis and would just like to forget about everything.

The eight of Leaves however advises a different behaviour. It indicates that you will soon regain your equilibrium and that everything will seem much easier and simpler and that the obstacles are not insurmountable.

Card upright: do not abandon a venture: it is about to be realized; useless preoccupations, even those regarding one's health.

Reversed: someone will delude you; a medical visit is advised; difficulties in buisness.

NINE OF LEAVES

In the middle of this picture, that illustrates the nine of Leaves, there is a great dark moth, with its' wings unfolded and on whose back can be seen the characteristic white design that distinguishes its' species. A Fairy is riding on its back and guides it in flight.

It is not a very reassuring figure and in fact it makes one shiver a little. The nocturnal moths, poor things, do not illict much sympathy unlike butterflies which are always admired.

When the serene and carefree Fairies have a nightmare, which the moth well represents, they know it is not a good omen but that it forewarns of anxiety, sad events, doubts and suspicions. They worry a lot therefore if this card appears in their oracle.

If you have extracted the nine of Leaves however, it is not necessary to cross your bridges before you have come to them!

It is not a particularly fortunate card but as its suit clearly states, it refers more to the mind, to the psyche, therefore it expresses above all the prudence you must have in your enterprises, making the best use of your intelligence.

For the most part anxieties and suspicions are caused by ignorance, by an erroneous evaluation of the facts and of persons. Therfore this card suggests prudence, reflection, discretion. Only in this way can you achieve your aims.

Card upright: with enough will you could transform the moth into a beautiful butterfly; a strange conversation will amaze you.

Reversed: unfavourable change; against your will, you will need to embark on something.

105

TEN OF LEAVES

This card depicts a entanglement of branches covered in large leaves, on which we note diverse Fairies, stretched out or leaning on their elbows. It is not a happy and vivacious scene as images of Fairy life usually are. It gives the impression of sadness or melancholy. Why are they immobile, these inhabitants of the magic forest who always seem to be restless? Are they sleeping or are they so worried by something that weighs them down and oppresses them that they remain there without the strength to act?

Both of these hypotheses are possible, as observing the suit of Leaves of this card we know that it refers to the sphere of the mind, the psyche and also to worries and sadness, which can make one unwell.

These magical and sensitive creatures unfortunately can also become sick and are more easily subject to psychosomatic illness than we are. When the Fairies extract the ten of Leaves they worry a lot because it indicates some event where it impossible for them to act, or else it forewarns of a physical illness.

The appearance of this card in your oracle therefore is not a favourable sign: it forewarns of a grave impediment, something that could block you, perhaps an obstacle created by your psyche, or an illness. The cards will make this clear.

Card upright: moral anxiety; doubts; obstacles placed by a third party; an illness.

Reversed: a forewarning. Avoid an obstacle, contracting a dangerous illness; it depends on you alone.

KNAVE OF LEAVES

The suit of this card indicates it belongs to the element of Fire, to the sphere of the mind. In the picture a Fairy with a sneaky and sly expression is standing amongst the flowers and the grass. He is wearing a uniform adapted for long walks in the forest. He has a lovely red feather high on his cap, a sword at the belt and in his hand he holds a halberd. Everything about this person makes one think of someone who is capable of slipping away between the trees without anyone noticing him, in order to eavesdrop without being seen.

This Fairy is indeed curious. The secrets of the others are not just for him but, on his return home, he greatly enjoys telling them to everyone.

For a Fairy, the appearance of the Knave of Leaves in their response indicates a friend, a young impartial man, perhaps interesting, with the superficiality of adolescence with a secret to tell, innocently and certainly not for money.

If you extracted this card in your oracle therefore, you will have dealings with a young person, who could be sincere and a friend, but in whom it is better not to confide: it would be the same as placing an advertisment in the papers!

It could also indicate the arrival of a reserved and confidential letter, the discovery of a secret, which could be important and favourable to you.

Card upright: do not confide rashly; do not betray the faith put in you; important news on the way.

Reversed: a secret of yours will be discovered; you have a person nearby who meddles too much in your affairs; a blackmail – more moral than material.

107

KNIGHT OF LEAVES

In the illustration of this card we see a Fairy riding on the back of a large red fox with a thick tail. Both the rider and the mount have a decisive, almost spirited air.

This bold youth, with his tall blue cap, carries a sword in his belt and holds a halberd in his hand.

We are looking at the Knight of Leaves who, even if the suit of Leaves directs us to the sphere of the mind, is an intelligent man, but one who is armed and able in battle. Frequently in fact, the best knights amongst the young Fairies, the more expert in the use of arms, choose combat as their profession, offering their services to whoever asks for it.

This card therefore does not have a positive nor negative meaning in itself, as all depends on the use, good or bad, that is made of the youthful energy and from the criteria for choosing the cause or for whom the Knight will fight.

The Knight of Leaves in your oracle indicates a young person who is energetic, full of vitality and who undertakes an active profession, perhaps an artist, a man ready for conquest. Keep in mind however the significance of the cards nearby: if negative this card could indicate a departure, a distancing, an immigration or even the breaking up of a relationship. If positive, it could mean a victorious battle, the attainment of your goals, overcoming obstacles, and the arrival of help, even if paid.

Card upright: energy and vitality used well; efforts well-aimed; an energetic and interested man will help you.

Reversed: a moment of weakness, lack of decisions that are wasted; an unfavourable move; be wary of offers of help.

QUEEN OF LEAVES

What spendid wings this lady of the Fairy people has, enough to make a butterfly jealous!

She wears an elegant and luxurious dress and her head is decorated with a gold threaded hat with a green border and a cluster of pearls at the top.

Between the flowering grasses, under a sky already darkening with night, she has a thoughtful air, a far-away glance. She does not even bother to use her fan which she holds in her hands, lost as she is in her mediations.

She has a vaguely melancholy air, that of a person who sees and thinks a lot but who prefers to not express their own thoughts.

For the Fairies the Queen of Leaves in their Tarot therefore represents a woman alone, independent, perhaps a little unusual but gifted with a good intellect. In any case she is honest and could be an affectionate friend, one who gives sensible advice when needed.

When this card appears in your oracle, it refers to an intelligent woman, educated, who could have your interests at heart. As this is a card of Leaves, where the suit refers to the intellectual sphere and to the mind, it can also indicate that you are experiencing a moment of melancholy. Your heart is a little sad or regretful and you would be better off talking about it so as not to make it seem bigger than it is.

Card upright: a good friend; useful suggestions; concrete support from a woman; satisfactory results from an undertaking.

Reversed: a shrewish woman, hostile; tendentious advice.

109

KING OF LEAVES

In the picture we see a wooden swing with a canopy above that is suspended in the air by a rope, where the King of Leaves is happily seated. It is a singular throne, but we are in the magic kingdom and Fairies don't tend to conform.

The symbol of Leaves represents the world of the intellect and the mind. The serious but serene expression of this person is of an intelligent and wise person, broadminded, due to the experiences of his life.

For the Fairies this card has a positive meanng. They know that it's appearance in their oracle announces authority acquired from either work or buisness. It is the symbol of a person who has risen by his own merits and intelligence.

If you extract the King of Leaves in your consulatation, congratulate yourself: it is an optimal prognosis. It refers in fact to a man with an acute and expert mind. It could even symbolize a father figure for you, or a person to whom you can turn with the same trusting spirit, certain of his kindness and understanding. More generally it represents the intelligence that enables realizations: therefore a wise person, an inventor, an artist, a person with a flair for buisness.

Card upright: success realized; fortune achieved; you are looking for a powerful protector, or else help from an important source.

Reversed: serious obstacles; unmotivated seriousness or irritations; reproaches from a person of authority.

110

ACE OF ACORNS

In the image of this card, a large acorn stands out in the foreground. Behind this we can see a lovely little pig seated with a tall violet hat on his head, decorated with gems, from which his ears poke out. He also wears a beautiful embroidered blue collar.

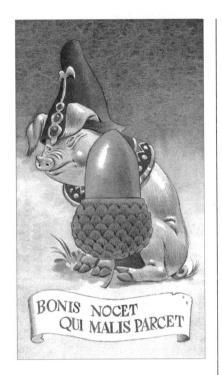

Acorns and pigs are both considered lucky charms in our real world, above all by the northern populations, but in the magic kingdom of the Fairies, they have an even more important significance.

Acorns are in fact a primary food for pigs, as they are for Fairies, especially in the winter. They are therefore a symbol of the struggle to survive, for the spirit of intiative and the creativity needed to overcome daily difficulties.

When the Ace of Acorns appears in the Fairy Tarot, it indicates for them the begining of an enterprise, but also the triumph of trust in oneself.

In your oracle this card could also indicate exaggeration: remember the greed of the pig for the acorns, therefore symbolizing something taken to extremes. Attention therefore to the totality of the card. If the other cards are positive and indicate prosperity and wealth, then the Ace of Acorns signifies maximum prosperity. If the other cards are negative then the prognosis clearly becomes less favourable.

Card upright: success of an undertaking; obstacles overcome, battles won.

Reversed: anger; many serious obstacles to be overcome; end of a relationship, even a sentimental one.

The writing that appears on the scroll is in Latin and reads: "Bonis nocet qui malis parcet". This can be literally translated as "He who spreads evil harms the good". As this refers to the Suit of Acorns one must not forget the exortation to action. The good must be careful of those who spread evil – above all under false pretenses – and fight them.

111

TWO OF ACORNS

The design of this card presents us with an opening in the forest, where two Fairies, a boy and a girl, are chasing each other, happy and carefree, around a tall large red-topped mushroom.

The two Acorns, at the top of the card, refer with their suit to the daily difficulties of life and to the methods needed to overcome them. Their number meanwhile symbolizes the antagonism of opposing forces, expressed also by the two Fairies.

We therefore have a clear indication of opposite tendencies, one against the other, about which even the carefree Fairies must meditate, as the choice is always difficult.

This uncertainty can also refer to their own abilities. Are their ways of dealing with life and the provisions made adequate or not?

When this card appears in your response, it reveals that you are going through a difficult time, many things seem stacked against you and you need time to refect or to evaluate carefully all the pros and cons.

The two of Acorns can also signify friendship or trickery, and you need to observe carefully not only the general response of the divination but especially the two nearest cards. These will provide the negative or positive sense of this card.

Card upright: small diffuculties that can be overcome quickly; help from friends; there is finally light at the end of the tunnel.

Reversed: rivalry; betrayal by friends; pain afflicted by others.

THE SUITES OF MINOR ARCANA

THREE OF ACORNS

The image presented in this card is very singular. We note in the center of the card an impressive Fairy, hands by his side, dressed in a beautiful red jacket with a crown on his head. He is surrounded by numerous Fairies, four of whom are dressed as pages and who are busy holding up the ends of his long whiskers and his equally long beard and hair.

When the three of Acorns appears in their response, the Fairies immediately know that they must have plenty of patience – all the patience that this person on the card had to have to keep all of his amazing hair!

This card therefore indicates the time necessary between the ideation of a project and its' realization. The interlude prior to the begining of a new enterprise is alway emotional and joyful.

The Fairies are always jovial but never unprepared and they do not mind if they need to wait to have good news, which encourages them in their activities.

If you have extracted this card, try to not to be impatient: do as the Fairies, even if they have the advantage over you of living for centuries, lucky things!

Card upright: positive news that you are expecting will arrive; you can begin your project; your wait will be rewarded.

Reversed: projects that fail; impatience or haste, that causes damage, errors in planning.

113

FOUR OF ACORNS

This card illustrates a scene of great serenity, which immediately fore-tells of a favouable response.

We see a large nest, almost hidden by a leafy branch, occupied by a Fairy, with a typical red beret on his head, sitting between two friendly solemn-looking owls. A bird with a long yellow beak is perched on the edge of the nest.

On the upper part of the card are four Acorns, to indicate both the numerical value of the card and to refer to daily life, and all its neces-sities.

The decisively satisfied expression on the face of the Fairy shows he is at ease and happy, in contact with nature, surrounded by the creature friends of his beloved woods.

Complete contact with nature is always the greatest desire of these inhabi-tants of the magic Kingdom.

The Four of Acorns, when it appears in your response, is therefore a good sign. It shows that you are experiencing a period of serenity and that your practical life, from work to matters of the heart, is also positive. It could announce favourable news, or occasions that you will be able to utilize well.

Card upright: an un-hoped for favourable occassion; news or positive con-firmation.

Reversed: still favourable, but what you wish for will not happen immedi-ately.

FIVE OF ACORNS

A white butterfly, flying overhead, observes some of the members of the magic Fairy people. It's curiosity has been noticed by a boy who is kissing the hand of a lovely girl. Both are on a large leaf, while nearby another Fairy is holding out his hand towards them in protest.

This scene clearly indicates rivalry in love, which is considered by the Faeries to be the most ruthless and hardest of competitions to withstand.

The Fairies are carefree and happy. They like to joke and play, but are also very sensitive. Love, whether for nature or for one of their kind, is always felt strongly, and is what involves them the most.

The Five of Acorns is a card that the Fairies regard therefore with apprehension when it appears in their response, as it always indicates a battle in some sector of their life, a grave and undesired commitment that they cannot get out of.

If you extract this card, be prepared to grit your teeth and to pull out all the determination you have and go into "attack mode", because a fight will be inevtable, in whatever area, and you will not be able to avoid this difficulty.

Card upright: inevitable conflict; loss or theft; fixed, obsessive ideas.

Reversed: be on guard against yourself; dangerous jealously from others.

115

SIX OF ACORNS

The image of this card is one of a rather unusual scene in the daily life of these magic people, fundamentally peaceful and accomodating.

We see in fact, in an opening almost devoid of vegetation, Fairies who are fighting each other. In the foregrund we see two contenders, totally armed, with feather helmets, armour, shields and long spears. In the background another pair of combatants can be seen.

When there is a very important or serious reason for disagreement, even the most well-balanced Fairies decide to use arms. It indicates a kind of tornament, as in the Middle Ages and this type of duel has only one absolute victor.

This card therefore is not a bad omen for the Fairies: extracting it in their Tarot announces without doubt a victorious battle!

If the six of Acorns appears in your oracle, you can expect a battle, a contest, a debate, even if you are not the instigator of this and wish only for tranquillity and peace. Console yourself that the victory, or the reason, will be yours.....

Card upright: you could eliminate an obstacle, even in the sentimental area; favourable outcome of a legal controversy; triumph of a project initially contested.

Reversed: malicious slander; gossip; moral, physical or sentimental impotency; a citation.

116

SEVEN OF ACORNS

In the background we see a lake, or the edge of a pond at the foot of a hill where a Fairy with a cheeky and satisfied expression rides on the back of a giant beetle (one of those that looks frightening due to the large horns pointing out from it's head).

This Fairy has good reason to be satisfied: his friendship or alliance with such a creature is undoubtably advantangeous to him in his daily life in the forest, which is not always without its dangers.

According to an old and valid principle, there is strength in union. The astute Fairies therefore search to procure valid support, secure alliances, and to sustain their own motives or projects.

The appearance of this card in their oracle warns them, as it indicates that at this moment, for one reason or another, their adversary is in a more advantageous position than they are, and that they must seek shelter if they do not wish to be defeated.

If you extract the seven of Acorns in your consultation therefore, do not loose time. Sharpen your wits, the situation is not as tranquil as it seems to be and those who wish to strike are well-trained. You will need all of your will and even outside support from friends or family, or a qualified and specific assistance.

Card upright: temporary success for a wicked person; unexpected betrayal; robbery; a danger.

Reversed: a success that costs a sacrifice; momentary victory, indisposition.

117

EIGHT OF ACORNS

The first impression one gets from looking at this card is amazement. We see in fact a long serpentine trail of Fairies, so long that you can't see the end of it. They are winding their way up a hill, leaning on long sticks and helping one another to overcome the ruggedness of the terrain.

It seems as if the entire magic Fairy population is on the move, but what has provoked this mass exodus?

It happens at times, luckily not often, that a part of the forest they have inhabited is no longer able to provide them with the resources necessary to sustain them, therefore the Fairies are obliged to move to another zone that is still lush and fertile.

Extracting the eight of Acorns therefore reveals to the Fairies that it is time to move on, and that any delay would be harmful.

If this card appears in your oracle, get moving at whatever cost, as it indicates that the action will be timely, whereas doing nothing will cause damage. In another sense it says that you can begin a new project, a new situation or that a parenthesis has closed and you are now free to initiate something else.

It can also indicate an interior change, the possibility to see a person or a situation in a different light.

Card upright: renewal; change; obstacles overcome; positive enterprise; a timely trip.

Reversed: a heavy situation that blocks you; obstacles; unexpected nuisances; a trip delayed.

THE SUITES OF MINOR ARCANA

NINE OF ACORNS

Between the trees and the leaves on the ground, we see some Fairies in the middle of a ring of mushrooms. A Fairy is seated on top of the largest one. He is sitting still and pays no attention to his companions. He seems immersed in a kind of apathy that isolates him from the rest of the world.

Summer has finished and winter is on the way. It is a particular moment for the Fairies, when some of them fall prey to a stange phenomenon: a profound melancholy that deprives them of the will to move, or the desire for company. A very bad state of affairs for a member of these magical people, generally emblems of vivacity and happiness.

To see this card appear in their response is not a good prognosis for a Fairy, who understands immediately that he will be constrained to forced inaction. The Nine of Acorns in your oracle therefore announces a stagnant period, a delay. You are advised not to make plans or projects, neither long-term or short. You must wait. Even if you are burning with the desire to move, to act, don't do it. Follow the suggestions of this card. You are in a delicate moment and could easily, due to impatience or impulsiveness, make a wrong move which you will regret later. Whether this refers to others or to yourself, the totality of the divination will make clear.

Card upright: delay in achievements; lack of incentives; incubation of an illnes;, prudence is advised.

Reversed: persistent delays; adverse destiny, someone is thinking about a vendetta.

TEN OF ACORNS

The picture that illustrates this card is entertaining and sweet. It shows a funny scene where we see two characters. A young Fairy is sitting on the ground and appears to be waiting happily for the arrival of a beautiful ladybug, with a red back and black polka dots, which is making its way towards him.

The Fairy has good reason to be happy. The ladybug is noted as a lucky charm and also anounces the arrival of spring.

The trials of winter are over, that period of worry and discomfort. The Fairies can begin laughing and joking again, carefree with their friends in the enchanted forest.

This card is therefore favourable, and when is appears in their oracle

the Fairies are immediately in good spirits. They know that they have left hard times behind and can begin to hope positively again for the future.

Has the Ten of Acorns appeared in your oracle? It is alway a fortunate card, a gurantee of successes near at hand for you.

You have left behind all that has afflicted you and worried you lately. After a dark night, the pink aurora anounces a sunny day ahead.

Card upright: success assured; hope that is realized; ideas that bear fruit; sure recovery from a serious illness.

Reversed: do not be impatient! Wait a few more beats and then you can sing with joy.

120

KNAVE OF ACORNS

The Fairy that we see at the center of this card does not have a very reassuring look. He is wearing a mask that almost covers his eyes and is too arogant, and self-assured to inspire sympathy.

He also intimidates a little with the mace that he holds under his arm and that he rests upon, plus the sword in his belt and the shield hanging from the other arm. He wears a tunic of thick and tawny fur, as is the brim of his large hat.

In their enchanted Kingdom, between winter and the begining of spring, the blood of the young Fairies beats harder and faster. They change their usually meek character a little. In harmony with the other creatures of the forest, the Fairies also strongly feel the reawakening of nature.

In consulting the Tarot, this card agitiates the younger Fairies somewhat, especially if they have already eyed a lovely female, as it announces a rival for the hand of their beloved. For those who do not have a sentimental aim however, it could announce a messenger has arrived.

The Knave of Acorns in your response is never a good omen, as it also indicates a rival for you, an opponent, and not only in love. It actually indicates a young ambitious person, not very sincere; a person to keep at a distance, or else an unexpected obstacle.

Card upright: that person is not a friend; bad news; a lesser person who is your enemy in disguise.

Reversed: a trap: a conspiracy planned to damage you; a disloyal opponent.

KNIGHT OF ACORNS

Poor Fairy! Notwithstanding his decisive aspect, the quiver on his back full of arrows, the bow in hand and that he is riding on the back of a beautiful fawn, this member of the magical people makes one feel a little sorry for him, as we can also see his ruined wings.

Amongst the many troubles and disasters that winter brings for the Fairies, not the least is the deterioration of their beautiful but also very delicate and fragile wings. When this happens, the Fairies decide to leave. Undoubtably a more gentle climate could help them....

If they extract this card in their answer, the Fairies know that the moment has arrived to depart, to undertake a long trip, far away to a remote place, without hesitiation or remorse.

This card, when it appears in your oracle, urges you to drastic change. The life you are living is no longer indicated for you. You have adopted some bad habits or, without wanting to, you are perhaps frequenting damaging company.

The Knight of Acorns therefore also proposes an activity undertaken for an essentially practical reason. The Fairy that departs to save his wings could indicate therefore a lawyer, an athlete, a military person, a conqueror or even a woman. The true meaning will be enhanced by the other cards in the consultation.

Card upright: a timely trip; to win, action is needed; help in a difficult moment; precise identification of a treatment or cure.

Reversed: a dangerous trip; a vice that has the upper hand; danger of seduction; brutal aggression; culpable indulgence towards oneself.

THE SUITES OF MINOR ARCANA

QUEEN OF ACORNS

The lady represented in this picture does honour to the magic Fairy people. This Queen has enormous glorious wings and the decisive but cordial expression of a mature person who is very aware of herself. She firmly rests both her hands on the hilt of a long sword, with the point to the ground, and seems to sustain her. She is wearing a cloak of fur and even her crown is decorated in fur.

For the Fairies in their Tarot, the Queen of Acorns represents a serious, active and clever woman, who is not discouraged by the difficulties of life and ready to fight for what she believes in and for what she considers worthy of fighting for. This card refers to a person or an ideal: the friendship of a person of great value is to be aspired and conserved proudly once attained.

If you extract this card in your consultation, it is a favourable sign, as it reveals that a woman of some standing will be a friend. Most likely a single woman, perhaps a widow, who has not been made bitter by solitude. She is perhaps impoverished but rich in intelligence and in spirit. This is an important and precious friendship, that could be one of support and inspiration for you; an uncomparable help in the more difficult moments of life.

Card upright: moral and practical help, spiritual support; well-aimed advice. A good choice for a partner.

Reversed: your love is badly hidden; widowhood; a too authoritarian partner; an intriguing woman.

123

KING OF ACORNS

This card shows a typical winter scene, with tall pines, bare branches, white flowers and a white blanket of snow covering the ground. In the front we see a Fairy. In one hand he holds a long cape of fur and with the other he holds, almost as if it were a pole, a spectre of gold with an acorn on the top. On his head he has a tall fur hat girded by a crown. He has a dignified air, authoritative, however behind the mask that covers them, his eyes are friendly.

This is a mature person, and the Acorn suit of this card, on the edge of his clothes and on the spectre, are a clear reference to the dificulties of life and the methods used to overcome them. They indicate his experience and abilities in that area.

The inhabitants of the enchanted Kingdom have a great affinity with nature and its cyclical seasons. During winter they loose a little of their exhuberance and carefree ways. More serious and aware, they search for friendships and the wise counsel of an older person, impersonated in their Tarot by the King of Acorns.

If this card appears in your response, it indicates a person, known or to know, of a certain importance. Mature and wise, he will be a friend who gives guidance and help when necessary. It could be a man of the law, a priest, a person from the police force, a person who can be trusted to lean on; to ask advice from.

Card upright: impartial and balanced advice; a valuable warning; a mature claimant to a good social and financial position.

Reversed: an unfavourable lawyer, a hardened enemy; a fascinating man, used to being in charge; dangerous.

124

HOW TO CONSULT THE FARIES

125

12 DIVINATORY READINGS

First of all, do not consider the Fairy tarot as a simple game or just enter-tainment. Behind the lightheartedness an immense knowledge is hidden, a concealed seriousness. You are dealing with secret forces..... and with those you do not joke!
Choose a moment when you can quietly gather your thoughts while avoid-ing being distrubed by anyone. Place the deck of cards in front of you but do not immediately open them. Rest for a few moments in silence. If you wish, you could listen to some relaxing music. Open your heart to the voic-es that come from higher up and finally mentally express what it is you desire.

1 – THE ORACLE OF LOVE

Let us imagine that you wish to formulate a question regarding love. Take the deck of 78 Fairies and shuffle the cards seven times, slowly, keeping in mind your question. Never cross your legs, as this will impede the energy that must flow freely from the Fairies to you. Now take your deck of cards and place them as illustrated:

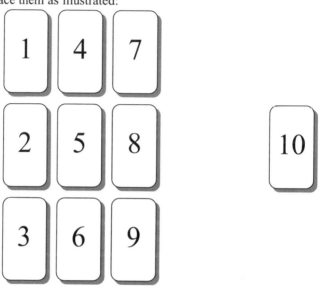

Place the first card high to the left
The second below it in a line
The third below this
The fourth next to the first
The fifth below that in a line
The sixth below this
The seventh high to the right
The eighth below this
The ninth below this in line
The tenth to the side, on the right

The three cards to the left refer to your past; those in the center to your actual emotional situation; those to the right to a meaningful future. The card on its own, to the right, represents the final outcome.

You have, for example extracted the following cards (the "C" indicates that the card appeared reversed).

1   The Tower
2   The Troll C
3   Ace of Bells
4   The Magician
5   The Empress
6   King of Hearts C
7   The Naiad
8   The World C
9   Queen of Hearts
10   The Sun

In the column refering to the past we find: the Tower, the Troll "C", and the Ace of Bells. This indicates that you have not been very fortunate in love. In the past you have had unhappy experiences due to incompatability of character or due to solitude.

The Tower indicates that your dreams of love have been shattered, as if destroyed by a stroke of lightening, similar to that of the Fairy of the XVI Arcana. Then we have the Troll, reversed, a horrid monster who lives near the barren rocks. He is nasty and jealous of other people's fortune. Finally the Ace of Bells is present, giving the strength needed to endure the more critical moments and showing the wider prospectives.

The centre column (the present), includes the Magician, the Empress and the King of Hearts "C". This configuration immediately appears positive. The Magician says that the strength is in you: you can put into practice whatever your heart desires, you have the means: use them! The Empress gives vitality and the strength to act. She makes you calm and understanding with respect to the person loved. The King of Hearts, even though reversed, is allied constructively with the Magician and the Empress, making the emotional relationship more stable and understanding.

The third column, that of the future, is composed of the Naiad, the World "C", and the Queen of Hearts. The Naiad is a spirit of the night: she clears away the clouds and allows you to see the starry sky. She is a good omen. The World guarantees success in equal measure but as it is reversed, there will be a slight delay. Finally we have the Queen of Hearts, a figure that is always on the side of lovers. The last card, the final outcome, is the Sun, who shines her light in your heart: this will clarrify any doubts and make you happy.

129

2 – ORACLE FOR THE COUPLE

This oracle uses only the 22 Major Arcana cards. In reality you will only have 20 Fairies at your disposition, as you need to first extract the Magician and the High Priestess from the deck. The Magician in fact represents the consultant, if a man, while the High Priestess is the symbol of the consultant if a woman.

Next place the cards in numerical order, reversed on the table, and then, as you should each time, try to collect your thoughts prior to begining the divination.

Mix the cards well and create five stacks of three cards each, placing them in front of you as illustrated below. The Magician and the High Priestess should be placed together in the centre.

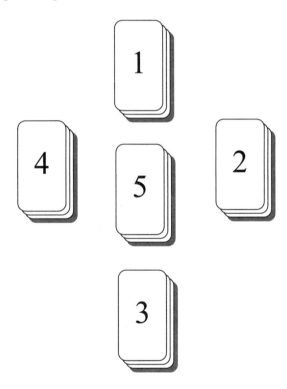

The first three cards are placed in position 1, the second three in position 2, etcetera. With the Magician and High Priestess in the centre there should be 17 cards on the table.

The first deck represents destiny – the karma of the couple; the second stack reveals how much freedom of choice you have; what you are able to do. The third stack indicates how your relationship is at present, the fourth reveals the obstacles from a third source/party, and the fifth reveals your future.

Now look at your cards.
As an illustration, you have chosen the following:
First stack- the Hanged Man, the Tower, and the Troll "C".
Second stack – the Oread, Strength, the World
Third stack - the Chariot, the Dryad, the Hermit
Fourth stack – the Emperor, the Hierophant, the Empress
Fifth stack – the Moon, the Sun, Judgement.

Response: in the first group, corresponding to that of destiny, we find three negative Fairies, above all the Troll "C", and that the actual emotional situation is everything but rosy. Do not despair however as in the second group there are only Fairies who are friends of humans. These will console and guide you. The third group confirms, with the presence of the Hermit, that you are not experiencing a good emotional relationship. However the Dryad and above all the Chariot anticipate the arrival of a better situation in the future. They know how to support you, and to help you avoid being pessimistic and unmotivated.
The fourth row is good, revealing that you have no real obstacles from outside capable of disturbing your love. The real problem is within you, and is emotional and psychological.
Finally the fifth row confirms your state of mind, above all due to the presence of the Fairy Moon. On the other hand, the Sun intends to give you joy and the judgement necessary to reason and to reflect.

Conclusion: with their oracle the Fairies say that if you love your partner, with a bit of trust on your part and sincere dialogue between you both, it can all return to how it was before. If you feel too doubtful however, follow the answer of the destiny row and leave your partner. You do not have to fear that you will be alone for long!

131

3 – ORACLE FOR FRIENDSHIP – THE CABBALISTIC TREE

The tree of life, or Cabbalistic tree, contains within it the great mystery of life and the connection between man and the Cosmos. Within cartomancy, it is one of the more complete and valid systems as much of the most secret and occult methods can be applied to this tree.

On the tree, 10 Divine Emanations are hanging, called the 10 Sephiroth in Hebrew. Observe the design: the first nine are ordered into three triangles. The tenth is the last card at the bottom.

1	The Absolute, the Heavens
2	Divine Wisdom
3	Supreme intelligence
4	Love, Compassion
5	Will, Strength
6	The beauty of the sentiments
7	Purpose
8	Health
9	Reality
10	The Earth

For this oracle only the Major Arcana are used. Put them in order and shuffle them well and then continue as usual. Open the cards in front of you in a fan-shape, leaving them upside down. Extract ten cards and place them on the table acording to the scheme shown above.

The first triangle is the mind; the second represents the emotions, and the third refers to reality.

For example, you have extracted:

For the first triangle: the Oread, the Moon and the Lovers. These reveal that friendships are very important for you and in this you have the support of the Oread. However you are fickle: you can at times loose very valid people because the Moon has a destabilising effect on you.

The second triangle is composed of the Empress, the Sun and the Fairy Elf "C". The oracle reveals that you have friendships of value or with high-ranking people. The Fairy "C" does not make you always aware of this. Therefore you must be objective and purposeful with yourself. Do not expect that something will be just given. Friendship means above all willingness and love.

132

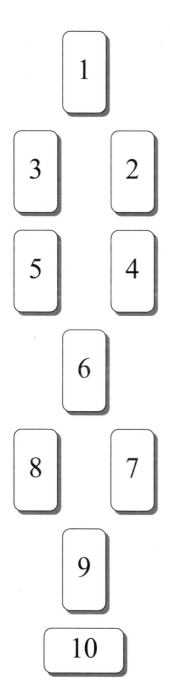

The third triangle is composed of the Emperor, the Hanged-Man "C" and the World. There is always someone who disturbs the harmony. In this case it is the Hanged-man "C", who makes you see things in a false light but who at the same time invites introspection and advises you not to make hasty decisions. The Emperor and the World however are with you.

The oracle concludes with the Sylph who promises serenity and joy in friendships. It depends on you however to make the right choices and to not be blinded by excessive or false praise or compliments.

133

4 – ORACLE FOR THE FAMILY

Shuffle the deck of the 78 Fairy cards as usual, and settle yourself in a state of inner silence. Do not let any thoughts disturb you.

When you feel sufficently serene and focused, take the prepared deck and make four stacks of four cards each in the following manner:

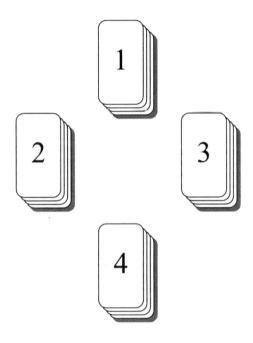

Begining with the first pile, deal out six cards, always face down and place the seventh on the table; then deal out the next six, placing the seventh again on the table, and continue as such until all four groups are completed.

At this point the first deck corresponds to one's personal situation, the second to your family, the third to contacts with one's acquired family and the fourth to your future.

Now turn over the cards. As an example, you have the following Fairies:

In the first stack: the Two of Bells "C", the Three and Four of Bells and the Emperor.

In the second stack: the Queen of Acorns, the Dryad, Seven of Leaves and Nine of Hearts.

In the third stack: the Hierophant, the Ace of Hearts, the Two of Hearts, the Knight of Leaves.

The Fourth stack: the Magician, the Knave of Acorns, the Six of Leaves and the Six of Hearts.

Your actual situation is a little turbulent: the Two of Bells "C" refers to a relative who is self-seeking, jealous and who tries to involve a person dear to you with false accusations and conjecture. However the Emperor represents the great inner strength that will guide you to a new harmony, if you are able to distance yourself from this jealous relative.

Within the immediate family circle all is going well. The four Fairies are good and affectionate. There are no clouds in the sky.

The third grouping represents your acquired family, and the outcome is mixed. There are at least two people who really wish you well, but another is at the least very opportunistic. You must therefore be careful and not believe in vain promises.

The fourth pile, that of the future, is rich with happy memories, the desire to travel and to do something unusual in the company of others. It is the Knave of Acorns who represents a young rather egocentric youth, while the Magician shows that it depends on your decisions if this youth manages to stop you more or less from being bored.

Finally, apart from small quarrels or momentary problems, you are fortunate in the area of family. And remember that even if moments of disharmony occur at times, what is important is that they are resolved immediately.

135

5 – ORACLE FOR WORK AS AN EMPLOYEE

Prepare the 78 Fairy cards in sequential order, from the first to the last card, begining with the 22 Major Arcana, from 0 (the Elf) to XXI (the World). Continue with the 14 cards of Hearts, from 1 to 10 then the Knave, Knight, Queen and King. Do the same with the 14 Bells, the 14 Acorns and the the 14 Leaves. The 78th card will therefore be the King of Leaves.

This sequence is the same for most of the oracles where the entire 78 cards are needed for the reading.

Place the deck face down in the table in front of you. Rest for a few minutes in silence, thinking about what you wish to know from the Fairies. You could perhaps listen to some background music if this assists you to relax more.

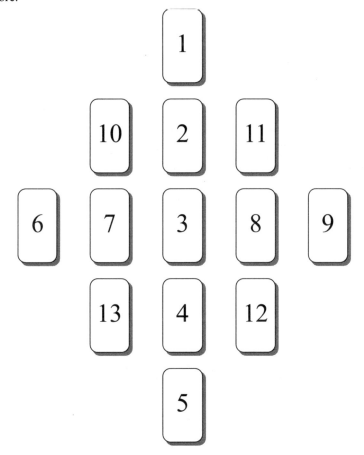

HOW TO CONSULT THE FARIES

Now take the entire deck in your right hand and leaving it face down, shuffle the deck well seven times. Then take from the top of the deck 13 cards, one at a time, and place them in front of you as in the diagram.

The scheme is composed of two crosses, a smaller one inside and a larger one outside. Diagonally there are a further 4 Fairies that are always interpreted as a couple: 10 –12 –11 – 13: these act as advisors and judges. The centre 3 serves as the final pronouncement.

Observe the following example:

1	The Moon
2	Naiad
3	Strength
4	5 of Leaves
5	Judgment
6	Sylph
7	Ace of Hearts
8	World
9	Death
10	2 of Acorns
11	Chariot
12	6 of Acorns "C"
13	3 of Hearts

The internal cross is composed of the Naiad XVII, Strength XI, the 5 of Leaves, the Ace of Hearts and the World XXI. The last card in particular indicates that you are very fortunate. Even if you loose your job (5 of Leaves), which probably does not give you satisfaction any more, you will find a better one. This is guaranteed by the Ace of Hearts, the World and the Naiad. Just as important is the final outcome of the central Fairy, symbolizing inner strength.

The diagonal from left to right is composed of the 2 of Acorns and the 6 of Acorns "C". The 2 is a Fairy that invites meditation and reflection. The 6 gurantees success after a brief period of struggle or rivalry with egocentric or jealous people. The other diagonal from right to left is composed of the Chariot and the 3 of Hearts. The Chariot promises sure success and the 3 will help evolve and grow spiritually.

The external cross, which represents that which comes towards us, is formed by the Moon, the Sylph, Death "C", and Judgment. It predicts a radical change in your actual work. The Moon is unstable and creates alternating emotions. The Sylph confers serenity and maximum inner harmony; Death, depending on your question, is intended as change here, as something that dies in order to allow for the emergence of something else. The Judgment invites introspection and to make a request or ask a favour on your behalf, provided that it is not to the detriment of others.

Nevertheless, if you are able to remain calm, thoughtful and aware, the Fairies will be with you to make your wishes come true.

6 – ORACLE FOR INDEPENDENT WORK

Prepare yourself in the usual manner prior to initiating the oracle. Utilize both the Minor and the Major Arcana, from which however you need to remove the suit of Hearts. The deck is therefore composed of 64 Fairies. Place the cards in front of you on the table in a fan-shape. Extract 7 cards and place them according to the following example:

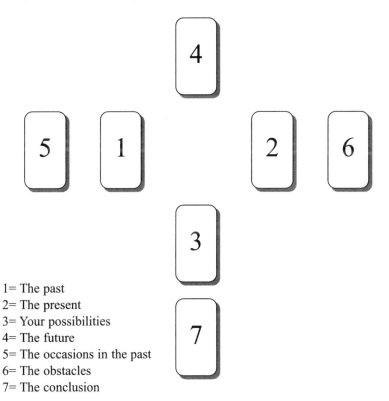

1= The past
2= The present
3= Your possibilities
4= The future
5= The occasions in the past
6= The obstacles
7= The conclusion

For example you have extracted:
1: The Knight of Leaves
2: The Empress
3: Then 4 of Leaves "C"
4: The World
5: The Knight of Acorns
6: The Naiad
7: The Queen of Bells

139

The Knight of Leaves reveals that you have had good success. Nevertheless, especially if you are very young, you have not understood the full importance of this, including certain advantages that as a consequence, did not last long.

The Empress promises satisfaction in the work area and will support you. You have many opportunities to improve your position if you are capable of not giving up the challenge, given that you are wanting to slow down the pace and retreat a little from the career race: a characteristic typical of the Fairy in the 4 of Leaves reversed. The future, with the World, is really rosy. The Knight of Acorns however indicates that you have, at least once, changed the direction of your work. You have travelled, worked in different places, wasted good opportunities, urged by a thirst for new things or from a lack of experience. Nonetheless you have managed to remake yourself.

The sixth position does not reveal obstacles, other than those you will come by your own hand, as the Naiad is a truly lucky Fairy.

The concluding card is one of the best: the Queen of Bells, who is magnificently generous, and will bring you much wealth not only thanks to work but also from other sources (for example a win at gambling or an inheritance).

140

7 – ORACLE FOR ONE'S ECONOMIC POSITION

Begin in the same manner, putting the 78 Fairies in order, mixing the cards and reflecting for a few minutes. Take the deck face down in hand then select the first, third, fifth, seventh, ninth, eleventh, thirteenth, fifteenth, eighteenth and twenty-first cards placing them according to the following diagram:

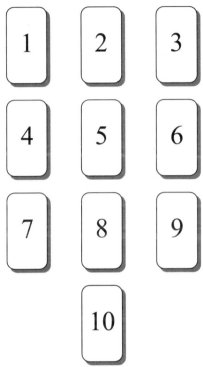

First line (1, 2, 3): What you had, or could have had
Second line (4, 5, 6): What you have at this time
Third line (7, 8, 9): What you will have in the future
Last card (10): The outcome

As an example, you have extracted:
First line: The Heirophant, the King of Leaves, the Knave of Hearts
Second line: The 4 of Leaves, the Oread, the King of Bells
Third line: The King of Hearts, the Naiad, the Moon "C"
Last card: The 2 of Leaves

The Fairies in the first line reveal that in the past you have had a successful job that was also well paid, but perhaps this seems logical and obvious. You also risked loosing good economic security. However you were saved because the second line, that of the present, indicates professional affirmation thanks to the Oread, and good earnings due to your own merit. In the future you can count on a solid financial base. The Naiad will not abandon you, while the reversed Moon could cause you to have a crisis due to new offers of work or minor speculations that you are not sure about. You would do well to not trust these!

The outcome, the 2 of Leaves, are good advisers and will protect you.

If you follow the dynamic suggested by the Fairies, you will have nothing to fear concerning your economic situation.

8 – ORACLE FOR THE YEAR

This oracle reveals the course of the whole year. Use all of the 78 cards, shuffle them as usual, placing them in numerical order from 1 to 78. Mix the deck well, at least seven times. Place the cards face-down on the table and rest in meditation for a few minutes.

Distribute the cards as shown in the diagram in next page and begin with the current month. Assuming we are now in March 2004, the cards will be valid until February 2005.

First line (odd numbered positions): the past
Second line (even numbered positions): the present

For example you have extracted:

March			September		
1	7 of Hearts "C"		7	Ace of Hearts	
13	Hanged man		19	Emperor	

April			October		
2	Queen of Bells		8	King of Acorns	
14	2 of Acorns		20	9 of Hearts	

May			November		
3	Ace of Leaves		9	Queen of Leaves"C"	
15	Empress		21	9 of Hearts	

June			December		
4	10 of Leaves		10	8 of Leaves	
16	4 of Leaves "C"		22	9 of Leaves	

July			January		
5	7 of Leaves		11	Queen of Acorns	
17	Ace of Acorns		23	5 of Bells	

August			February		
6	6 of Hearts		12	Knave of Hearts	
18	4 of Hearts		24	King of Hearts	

| 1 | 2 | 3 | 4 | 5 | 6 | 7 | 8 | 9 | 10 | 11 | 12 |
| 13 | 14 | 15 | 16 | 17 | 18 | 19 | 20 | 21 | 22 | 23 | 24 |

You have extracted only 3 Major Arcana cards, which indicates that your successes in every area depend largely on you, because the Major Arcana represent Destiny whereas the cards of the Minor Arcana leave plenty of room for our decisions and actions.

Begin the reading with the month in which you are asking the oracle. Analyze each month seperately:

March: the 7 of Hearts reversed places you on alert: unpleasant situations due to some wrong move could be verified. The Hanged man will certainly not help you and you will be more pessimistic. Listen to the Fairy 7 of Hearts and you could get out of this, only if you remain cautious enough.

April: a favorable month. The two positive Fairies and the Queen of Bells will support you and will be useful, but do not conceed to the excessive stimulus of the 2 of Acorns. They are good Fairies but always thoughtful and tend to reflect endlessly. Do not listen to them as you could become so confused as to not know whom to listen to anymore.

May: a month rich with promise. The Ace of Hearts is always generous and the Empress knows what she wants, This will be a beautiful period for you. If you have a wish you can realize it now with the help of these two Fairies.

June: be careful of changes in temperature, you could get a kind of influenza: nothing serious but annoying, thanks to the 4 of Leaves reversed. A slower pace than usual from the multiple jobs to do will do you good. You will find the time to read a good book or listen to some pleasant music.

July: this month seems especially dedicated to professional issues. You have extracted two hard-working Fairies. You could lay the background for new projects, that will begin with good omens. You have very little free time to think about a holiday, even love comes off second-best: do not overdo it!

August: finally a little rest; a good chance to meet up with new and old friends: the 6 and 4 of Hearts are extrovert, friendly. This is therefore a restful month but also entertaining. Important issues regarding love also come into play, but do not be too trusting: not everyone will be sincere with you.

September: you have again extracted the Fairies of Hearts, therefore love is once more in first place. The Ace of Hearts is lucky: what more could you wish for? If you are still single, you could meet the partner just for you.

October: two Fairies represent mature men who will stand by you. Work and friendship also come into play, not only love. Willingly or not, you must begin to think about your usual obligations and daily tasks, however no need to worry, you will be well supported.

November: everything is getting better. Things are proceeding in the right way, but notwithstanding this you tend to have dark thoughts, as the reversed Queen of Leaves is a Fairy who feels alone and at times unhappy. Rely on the 9 of Hearts who will bring you joy and optimism, as well as new future prospectives.

December: the 8 and 9 of Leaves indicate disatisfaction. You will feel dominated by melancholy and memories which will easily disturb you. From a work point of view, all goes well, but you do not feel in good shape psychophysically. Perhaps you have worked too hard; stress produces negative thoughts. Help yourself with relaxation techniques, for example autogenous training.

January: the Queen of Acorns represents a good friend, or mother, who you can always count on. Unfortunately in this moment she is accompanied by the 5 of Bells, who is a bright Fairy but with no heart. She anounces an emotional break or the distancing of a dear person. In the previous month you were melancholy and sad without an apparent motive. Perhaps you had a premonition of painful moments to come. It is said however that not all bad things have bad endings. If you are dealing with an emotional rupture prehaps in the future you will even be content about this.

February: this month closes our inquiry. It presents us with two optimistic cards: the Knave and the King of Heart. You will be supported, and will have proof of esteem and affection, which will help you exit the dark state you have been in. Life will return smiling!

9 – THE ASTROLOGICAL ORACLE

This system is one of the more complete, as it can give a response regarding all sectors and between events that are verified as they are occuring.
In astrology the zodiac circle is subdivided into 12 parts, called Houses, each one of which corresponds to an aspect of our terrestrial experience:

1st house: character, tendencies, personal talents
2nd house: economic situation, earnings, losses
3rd house: brief trips, relatives, interpersonal relationships
4th house: parents, close family, end of life
5th house: love, children, art, types of entertainment
6th house: dependent work, health
7th house: marriage, living together, buisness partners, legal issues
8th house: inheritance, existential crisis, occult world
9th house long trips, superior studies, overseas contacts
10th house: career, notoriety, worldly life, social life
11th house: friendship, ability to judge, hope
12th house: adversity, hidden enemies, closed doors, introspection

The Major Arcana only is used.
Prepare the cards in the usual way, shuffling them and placing them face-down on the table from left to right.
Place the 13th and 14th cards in the center. They will be the final outcome.
Put the other cards to one side.

For example, you have chosen the following cards:
1st: the Chariot
2nd: Strength
3rd: the Hierophant
4th: Death
5th: the Hanged Man
6th: the High Priestess
7th: the Elf
8th: the Emperor "C"
9th: the Naiad
10th: the Sylph
11th: the Lovers
12th: the Sun
The final outcome are the Oread and the Dryad

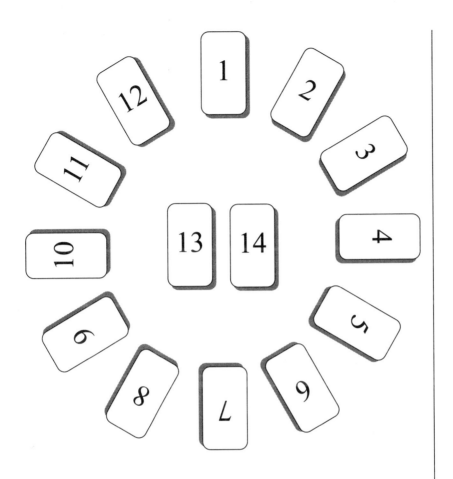

Interpretation:

1st house: the Chariot reveals that you are in great shape, enterprising and sure and believing in your own decisions and actions.

2nd house: Strength: this card confrms your vitality and your desire to dedicate yourself to diverse contemporary activities.

3rd house: the Hierophant gives his benediction, therefore go ahead.

4th house: you are suddenly slowed down in your tracks. Death reveals a danger for the health of a parent or a change in residence or work.

5th house: the Hanged man anounces that destiny will oblige you to change direction, in a way for which you are not prepared.

6th house: the High Priestess will enable you to brilliantly overcome a small crisis and you will find yourself better off than before.

7th house: the Elf creates ambiguous situations between couples and uncertain situations with buisness partners: be careful!

8th house: the reversed Emperor will give his support if you find yourself in an occult house. You must however act correctly and trust in the value of spirituality. A possible inheritance contested.

9th house: the Naiad promises interesting travels; if you are still studying you will not have difficulties and you will obtain good results. Your hopes will find the right moment to be realized.

10th house: the Sylph will show herself to be your friend. You will be successful at work.

11th house: the Lovers reveal that you will have proof of love from friends and from those who are near you.

12th house: the Sun will liberate you from every problem.

The final outcome, the Oread and the Dryad will guarantee their support in all predicaments.

Even if something occurs that upsets you greatly, the totality of this oracle is positive. Many Fairies will be nearby in times of trouble and there is much joy to be had just around the corner.

10 – ORACLE FOR HEALTH

Prepare yourself as usual with the deck well ordered: extract 15 Fairies and place them in front of you in the following manner:

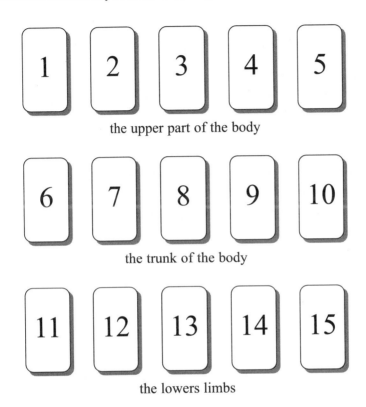

the upper part of the body

the trunk of the body

the lowers limbs

You have extracted, as an example, the following:

For the upper part of the body: the 6 of Bells, the Knight of Bells "C", the World"C", the Knight of Acorns, the 6 of Acorns.

For the trunk of the body: the Knight of Acorns, the 3 of Acorns, the Knight of Leaves, the 9 of Leaves, the Knave of Bells and the Naiad.

For the lower limbs: the Magician, the Chariot, the Elf"C", the Lovers and the 5 of Leaves"C".

149

Interpretation:

The upper part of your body is more than healthy. You could at the most have a little heaviness because at this time you really do have a lot on your mind!

The cards for the trunk indicate that there is no danger of a serious illness. You could however fall prey to anxiety: you always think the worse even if it is the slightest thing, whereas you have extracted the Naiad who will guarantee you good health.

For the lower limbs however, be careful. Do not take up dangerous sporting activities at this time and do not run. Tarvel either on foot or in a car. The reversed Elf and the reversed 5 of Leaves reveal that if you do not protect yourself against risks you could incur some small fracture, not a serious thing but annoying. The Magician offers a supporting and protective arm. Find time to rest more. With your head in the clouds it is easier to fall.

150

11 – ORACLE FOR A SPECIFIC SITUATION

The Major Arcana only are used.
Extract from the deck the Fairy that corresponds to your situation:

For a question of love: the Lovers
For a question of work: the Emperor
For a question regarding the family: the Sun
For an economic question: the Chariot
To win at a game/gambling: the Magician
For health: the Hermit
For spiritual evolution: the High Priestess

Prepare yourself in the usual manner and then divide the remaining Fairies
into three stacks of seven cards each:

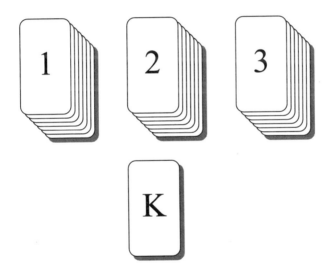

Your question regards love.

The Key card (K) is then the Lovers.

The first set:
The Sun - The Empress - The Troll - The Magician - Judgment - The Hermit
- The Tower

The second set
the Moon - Strength - the Chariot - the Heirophant - Death - the Hanged man - the High Priestess

The third set
the Elf - the Emperor - the Naiad - the Sylph - the World - the Oread - the Dryad

The first set refers to the past, the second to the present and the third to the future.

The past speaks of a brief passionate love affair which ended unexpectedly, thanks to the Troll. It left you profoundly disturbed. After a long period you fell once again in love, but this also finished badly, as shown by the Tower, which caused your dreams to come crashing down.
The second set show you have begun a new romance, thanks to Strength, the Heirophant, the High Priestess and the Chariot. It seems that fortune has arrived, but alas the Hanged Man and Death have also put an end to this relationship, or it could be that you are in the midst of a crisis as it is about to end. This is probaby a karmic debt. The causes are due to a third party.
The third set, that of the future, is wonderful: nothing will stand in your way. The Arcana IV, XVII, XIV, XXI, X, and VIII will bring you lots of joyous love. The Fairies will inebriate you with fantasy, vital energy and love.

Therefore you are currently in crisis for your actual emotional situation but try not to despair and try not to keep alive something that is not there anymore. Have faith in the Fairies. They promise you a partner who will know how to make you happy.

152

12 – THE KEY OF FORTUNE

Prepare yourself in the usual manner, using all of the 78 cards, however make two piles, one with the Minor Arcana and the other with the Major Arcana.

When you are ready and the cards have been mixed well, take the first five cards from the Major Arcana and another five from the Minor Arcana and place them as follows:

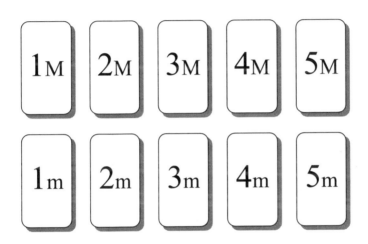

Major Arcana: 1M, 2M, 3M, 4M, 5M
Minor Arcana: 1m, 2m, 3m, 4m, 5m

The first vertical pair are the errors from the distant past; the second the more recent past; the third the present, the fourth the future and the fifth the key that will make you happy.

As an example you have extracted the following:

Major Arcana: XII, VIII, XVII, I, X
Minor Arcana: 6 of Acorns, Knight of Acorns, 8 of Hearts, 4 of Leaves, Ace of Leaves.

The first couple, the Hanged Man with the 6 of Acorns, speak of a painful past: you have struggled for your serenity and a certain security, but exter-

153

nal events did not leave you free to choose. In a way you have won the battle anyway, your character having been much strengthened along the way.

The second couple, the Dryad and the Knight of Acorns, indicate that you have managed to adapt yourself, even in delicate matters, and to be far-sighted.

The present, with the Naiad and the 8 of Hearts, shows you already have the key and this comes to you from the stars. It is important that you realize this and that you don't go looking for other explanations.

In the future, the couple formed by the Magician and the 4 of Leaves bestow on you a particular strength and a magic charisma. Happiness will be within you. Don't waste time looking for it externally!

The key is presented to you by the Oread and the Ace of Leaves, Fairies who love people and whom together have many gifts to give. This means therefore that victory in all areas will arrive! With the wisdom and ability to draw from the resources that are within you, you will find the key to your success and serenity.

AUTHORS

155

HELENE SALTARINI

Helene G. Kinauer Saltarini, was born in Vienna but has been living in Italy for many years. She graduated in Psychology at the Jolla University in San Diego (California, USA), and she is the author of several Astrology and Tarot books and essays.

She is also a common presence and author in many magazines, radio and television shows on the subjects of Astrology, Tarot and Occult Psychology.

RICHARD DOYLE

(London, U.K. 1824-1883), the second born of John Doyle, a caricaturist for the famous satyrical magazine "Punch", instructed his son so well in the art of design and illustration that as an adolescent Richard published a book "The Eglington Tournament", which had a considerable success. He was an accomplished painter and one with a great imagination (his works were exhibited at the Royal Academy in 1866 and 1871 and at the Grosvenor Gallery). He dedicated himself above all however to the world of elves and his drawings appeared in the stories "King of the Golden River" by John Ruskin (1851) and "In Fairyland" by William Allingham (1870). The illustrations for the numerical cards of the Minor Arcana come from this last book.

ANTONIO LUPATELLI

Born in Busseto (Parma, Italy) in 1930, Lupatelli is certainly one of the greatest contemporary Italian illustrators of the fantasy genre. He made his debut in 1958 with a story board for animated cartoons for the French Payot Film, which were followed by illustrations for childrens' books for Fleetway of London. Since 1961 he has worked for the Italian company Fratelli Fabbri Editors, creating didactic drawings for scholastic texts and illustrations for books of fairytales. With Dami Editors, beginning in 1978, he has produced numerous books under various pseudonyms. For Art Editions of Lo Scarabeo he had designed five splendid decks: "Tarot of the Gnomes", "Tarots of Good Eating" ," The Zodiac of the Gnomes", "Celtic Tarots" and the "Fairy Tarot". His illustrations - fantastic, happy, ironic and colourful - are the cover signature for this volume as well as the Major Arcana, the Aces and the Court cards and Suits.

157